**60** Seconds

One of America's foremost career authorities, Robin Ryan is the best-selling author of five books: *24 Hours to Your Next Job, Raise, or Promotion*; *Winning Resumés*; *Winning Cover Letters*; *Job Search Organizer*; and *60 Seconds & You're Hired!* Robin Ryan has appeared on over 500 TV and radio programs, including the *NBC Nightly News* and *The Oprah Winfrey Show*. She's a frequent commentator on the CNBC television network and on Seattle's KIRO-TV News and KOMO Radio. A constant contributor to US national magazines and trade publications, she's been featured in *Money, Newsweek, Fortune, Glamour, Business Week, Cosmopolitan, Good Housekeeping, Mademoiselle, Women's Day*, and *McCall's* to name a few. She's appeared on the pages of most major US newspapers, including the *Wall Street Journal*, the *New York Times*, the *Los Angeles Times, National Business Employment Weekly*, and the *Chicago Tribune*. She is a career columnist for *women-CONNECT.com*—the largest business and career Internet Web site for women—and also a columnist for the *Seattle Times*.

Robin Ryan has spent a lifetime dedicated to helping people find rewarding jobs. A highly sought after speaker, she frequently talks to college alumni groups and at association conferences. With 15 years of hiring responsibility, Robin also teaches hiring seminars to employers. Additionally, her work includes assisting employers with outplacement situations.

A licensed vocational counselor for 20 years, she has an active career-counseling practice in Seattle where she offers telephone consultations to assist clients with resumés, interviews, salary negotiation, and other career issues. She holds a master's degree in counseling and education from Suffolk University and a bachelor's degree in sociology from Boston College, and is the former director of counseling services at the University of Washington. You may contact Robin Ryan at (001-425) 226-0414.

60 Seconds & You're Hired!

Robin Ryan

Vermilion
LONDON

3 5 7 9 10 8 6 4 2

First published in US by Impact Publications 1994
This expanded edition first published in the US by Penguin Books 2000

This edition first published in the UK in 2001 by Vermilion,
an imprint of Ebury Press, Random House,
20 Vauxhall Bridge Road, London SW1V 2SA
www.randomhouse.co.uk

Addresses for companies within The Random House Group Limited can be found at:
www.randomhouse.co.uk/offices.htm
The Random House Group Limited supports The Forest Stewardship
Council (FSC®), the leading international forest certification organisation.
Our books carrying the FSC label are printed on FSC® certified paper.
FSC is the only forest certification scheme endorsed by the leading
environmental organisations, including Greenpeace. Our
paper procurement policy can be found at
www.randomhouse.co.uk/environment

Printed and bound in Great Britain by Clays Ltd, St Ives PLC

The Random House Group Limited Reg. No. 954009

A CIP catalogue record for this book is available from the
British Library.

ISBN 0 09 185685 X

To my husband, Steven—

You always used to say I was the best job getter you know. Your support and encouragement have been vital in my mission to share my information with others. May they find a career as rewarding as mine.

And to Jack—

One of the greatest blessings God has ever given me is you, my son.

Preface

Can This Book
Help You Get Hired?

60 Seconds & You're Hired! made the *National Business Employment Weekly* best-seller list because it was an excellent resource to help guide people through the interview and salary negotiation process. I continuously received success story after success story that this book helped job hunters land great jobs. Originally written in 1994, it contained the best advice possible on this process. Over the years hiring trends change, and so I felt an updated book was needed. I had conducted new research—important changes that I've added to this book. This updated edition contains new facts, research, and client-proven strategies—30 percent more than the original. It's still concise, so you can read it in its entirety and use it the night before your interview. Everything you need to know to do your best in your next interview is covered. I hope you find this book the best resource possible, because my goal is to help you land the job of your dreams. When you do, let me know, and tell me what worked for you.

To your success—

Robin Ryan

Acknowledgments

A big thank-you to every job hunter who has worked with me or who has attended my seminars. They are why I wrote this book, and helping them is the driving force in my life. Many thanks to all the hiring managers who willingly gave of their time and expertise to add the best information possible to this book. Professionally, I'm grateful to Tracy White, who started my seminar business years ago when she first hired me to teach job hunting skills to CPAs; her continued support and assistance have been an important contribution in my career.

Thanks to Dawnelle Thompson and Mary Lynne Finn, who wonderfully typed all my changes to this manuscript; to Cindy Hurst, Mike Hurst, Steve Ryan, Jim Mullen, and Sandy DeHan, who all willingly read this book and offered valuable insights to improve it; and to Bob Holman, for his great project and time-management tips.

I am grateful to Pat Lowe for the wonderful care she gives my son so I can devote some time and energy to the work I love best. Thank you to Dr. Bob Bjurstrom, who offered incredible support and help during my illness, reinforcing the hope that I would again enjoy all aspects of my wonderful work—he was right, and I will be forever grateful for his encouragement and commitment to make it so.

My agent, Shelley Roth, is the best there is. I will always be indebted to her for her enthusiastic support. I am grateful to my editor, Jane von Mehren, for believing in and endorsing this book so wholeheartedly.

Above all else, my husband, Steven, has always believed in me and helps me with his great ideas—I'm so lucky to be his wife. My friends—Sarah, Cindy, Wendy, Peggy, Darlene, Martha, Ed, Azriela, and MJP—stood by me and offered "You can do it" when times got tough. They are the best cheerleaders anyone could ask for. My baby son Jack's smile and happy nature remind me of all the wonderful possibilities in life and all the promise that lies within each and every person.

Lastly, I'm grateful to my parents for raising me to believe that with determination, dedication, and enthusiasm you can achieve any goal you can dream of.

Contents

60 Seconds & You're Hired!

*Believing in yourself is
the starting point.
Effectively communicating
your abilities to others
is the necessity.*

Chapter 1

Why 60 Seconds?

We would like you to come in for an interview." Those wonderful words are what every job hunter wants to hear. Once they are said, a vision of landing the job starts to form in the job hunter's mind. When you get that call you hang up the phone, excited and pleased that your resumé has gotten you this far.

On the other end of the phone sits the employer who decided to call you in for an interview. Three thoughts are running through his mind: *Can you do the job? Will you do the job? Will you work out in their organization so they can manage you?* The employer is worried. It's hard to find a person who'll be a good fit. The workload is piling up; the pressure is on to make a good hiring decision. The employer hopes that you'll be "the one." He reiterates the important job duties he needs done. He's feeling anxious, hopeful, and skeptical all at once. He's praying that you have the skills to do the work.

For the employer, hiring is a difficult task. Mistakes can be very costly. Employee turnover often costs three times the person's salary, when adding in the loss of work, expense of errors, and training a new person. The employer wants to find the right person—quickly. He looks for someone who

3

can and will perform the job well. He looks for an answer to the problem of whom to hire.

There are several compelling reasons why the 60 Seconds approach is the ideal way to get your points across and convince an employer to hire you.

Attention Span

In today's fast-paced world, we often focus on things for less than 60 seconds. Verbose, lengthy answers, where job hunters babble on and on when answering interview questions, bore the interviewer into not hiring them. Nervousness and no preparation often result in long, continuous, never-ending answers.

The most effective way to capture attention is to use your enthusiasm to answer each question succinctly in a concise, brief manner. And never use more than 60 seconds on any answer.

Are They Listening?

Job hunters are amazed to learn that interviewers can ask them an hour's worth of questions and never hear any of the answers. Why? Because they aren't listening. They are tired, distracted, and bored, and feel the candidate is the wrong choice—that he or she can't do the job. When you get your point across in 60 seconds or less, you increase the odds that the person will listen. When you add specifics of how you've accomplished the needed tasks before, show support materials and work examples, and add vocal variety and enthusiasm to your answers, the employer starts to wake up and take notice. And when you put into practice two proven techniques you'll learn in this book—the 5 Point Agenda and the

60 Second Sell—the whole process takes on a new shape. The employer begins to get *excited* that she may have found the right person for the job—YOU!

The World Is Full of Sound Bites

Television and radio have filled our world with 30- and 60-second commercials—short, concise commercials that quickly get their points across. News reports use the same principles, limiting stories to one- to three-minute segments. We are all conditioned to these speedy communication tools. During a job interview, utilizing the right words that effectively get your message across concisely will build the employer's confidence that you can do the job.

Your Verbal Business Card

The 60 Second Sell is your basic tool to create interest with an employer. This 60-second calling card will summarize your skills, abilities, and previous experience in a well-thought-out fashion that will immediately make the employer want to listen. The 60 Second Sell is a proven shortcut to your success. Client upon client has reported it was the best job-search technique they'd ever used. It's easy to create and easy to implement. Once you've learned this technique, your interviews will be greatly improved because you will have done the most important thing necessary to land a job—get the employer to listen to you while you're telling him exactly how you can perform his job.

In the end,

what does any work mean to me?

That I have done my best,

excelled where I could,

taken risks,

and made a difference by being here.

Chapter 2

5 Point Agenda

The 5 Point Agenda is a method by which you can focus your interview on your strengths as well as break through the monotony and disinterest, and get the employer to listen. It is a hiring strategy created to focus on the needs of the employer and the job to be done. The 5 Point Agenda is a predetermined analysis in which you select your five most marketable points and and repeatedly illustrate these points throughout the interview process. It is this repetition and reiteration of exactly how you'll meet her needs that allows the employer to remember something about you. Clients have tested this interview approach with the following results:

- It made interview preparation easier.
- They were highly rated by everyone who interviewed them.
- The five points seemed to be all that was remembered.
- They credited the 5 Point Agenda and the 60 Second Sell as being the two techniques that secured the job offer.

Job hunters are often amazed to learn that an interviewer can ask you an entire hour of questions and not hear one word you've said. He may be bored, frustrated, or unimpressed with your image within the first few answers. After interviewing several people, all the candidates begin to blend together. I experience this when I hire people, and countless other employers continuously confirm this fact. The 5 Point Agenda captures an employer's interest because you are continually emphasizing exactly how you *can* do the job right from the start.

The Formula: Creating Your Strategy

Examine your previous experience. Write out the major responsibilities for each job you've held. Note any special accomplishments. Zero in on your important work strengths—those abilities where you are most productive.

Then, check with your contacts and use your network to get as much background as possible about the employer, the company, and the position's needs. Many times, your contacts will point out the very aspects that must make up your 5 Point Agenda. Other times, there will be little information available and you will need to guess based on your general knowledge about doing the job.

After reviewing the employer and position needs, determine which of your abilities and which aspects of your experience will be most important *to the employer*. Then create your 5 Point Agenda, selecting each point to build a solid picture emphasizing how you *can* do the job.

Three Examples

Let's examine three 5 Point Agendas that clients used during the interview process to land their new jobs. The jobs they applied for were chief financial officer, events planner, and engineer.

Chief Financial Officer

This position was with a rapidly growing international company needing strong financial and operations management. Here are the points the candidate came up with:

- Point 1: Fifteen years in senior financial management, directing international business start-ups, expansions, and turnarounds.
- Point 2: Took start-up manufacturer from zero to $38 million in 18 months.
- Point 3: Achieved corporate profitability goals at last five positions, and exceeded goals at four.
- Point 4: Hired more than 3,500 employees, uniting diverse workforce into cohesive productive teams.
- Point 5: Management Information System expertise in hardware, software, network conversions, and transportation, accounting and distribution systems.

It's important to note that the last point was simply a guess at the company's perceived need. During the interview process, this client realized that computer systems were a crucial need for this employer and was able to offer specific examples of his experience using management information systems to positively affect the bottomline at companies he had worked for previously.

Events Planner

The association needed a person with strong computer skills and previous event planning experience. As a new college graduate, this candidate created her 5 Point Agenda from her internship and part-time jobs:

- Point 1: Proficient PC and Macintosh computer skills with expert Internet capabilities.
- Point 2: Desktop publishing using Pagemaker; creating brochures, programs, invitations, flyers, press releases, training materials, and website updates.
- Point 3: Assisted with numerous special events, conferences, lunches, receptions.
- Point 4: Responsible for catering, food preparation, audiovisual setup, transportation, budget, expense reimbursements.
- Point 5: Acquired service bids from several contractors, caterers, hotels.

Engineer

This major automotive manufacturer required experience in both quality assurance and new product design. The candidate's 5 Point Agenda was:

- Point 1: Implemented new four-year quality-assurance program which received a national Quality-1 Award.
- Point 2: Effectively dealt with employee resistance to quality improvements.

- Point 3: Conducted 37 supplier on-site inspections to improve the quality of parts received.
- Point 4: Five years' design engineering experience.
- Point 5: Excellent communication skills when working with both technical and nontechnical staff.

Summary

Before every job interview, you will customize your 5 Point Agenda, responsibilities of the job as well as the company's goals and objectives. These five points are your basic building blocks to answer the interviewer's questions. You'll want to restress each of these points whenever the opportunity presents itself. The message the employer will hear is that you have the ability to perform and do well in the job—and it will give your prospective boss confidence in hiring you.

You'll never know
what you can achieve
until you try.

Just never, ever give up.

Chapter 3

60 Second Sell

The 60 Second Sell is a tool that helps you target your skills to meet the employer's needs. It allows you to summarize your most marketable strengths in a brief and concise manner. Successful job hunters have found that the 60 Second Sell is the most influential tool they used during the interview process. They praised the tool for several reasons:

- It was effective in capturing the employer's attention.
- It provided excellent, concise answers to tricky questions.
- It was very easy to use.
- It was a great way to end an interview.

The 60 Second Sell is a 60-second statement that you customize for each interview and that summarizes and links together your 5 Point Agenda. You will want to put each point of your 5 Point Agenda into an order that allows you to present them in a logical and most effective manner. When you link the ideas into sentences, they should be spoken in 60 seconds or less. Once memorized, this statement will be easy for you to recall and use during the interview.

When to Use It

Most interviews are over before they ever really get started. What should you do to avoid this trap? Immediately capture the employer's attention and get him tuned in to you as a true top-notch candidate. You need to open the interview by using your 60 Second Sell. Very typically the first question you are asked in an interview is *Tell me about yourself*. In an interview I recently conducted, I got a 20-minute answer. After the first minute or two, the prospect totally lost my attention. Had the person answered with a 60 Second Sell, he might have started the interview by grabbing my attention and keeping it. Questions such as *Tell me about yourself* require a brief summary noting your most marketable skills, not a life story.

Another question to which your 60 Second Sell is the perfect answer: *Why should I hire you?* This question is asking you to convince the employer to hire you. Other applicable inquiries include: *What are your strengths? What makes you think you are qualified for this job? What makes you think you will succeed in this position? Why do you want this job?* These questions offer you an excellent way to stress your 5 Point Agenda (your most marketable skills) using your 60 Second Sell.

The 60 Second Sell is effective because it demonstrates your strengths and illustrates how you will fill the employer's needs. That is the key to its success, and yours.

Three Examples

To clearly understand how your 5 Point Agenda is linked and becomes your 60 Second Sell, let's continue with our three earlier examples; here is how the candidates took their

5 Point Agenda and linked the points together to summarize them and create their 60 Second Sell.

Chief Financial Officer

This international company was in a rapid expansion phase that required expertise in financial as well as operational management. This candidate's 60 Second Sell stressed how he'd done it before:

"I have 15 years in senior financial management directing business expansions, start-ups, and turnarounds in the international arena. In my last three positions, I achieved corporate profitability goals and exceeded goals in two of those situations. For example, I took a start-up manufacturer from zero to $38 million in 18 months.

"I base my success on two abilities. The first is my ability to hire excellent people and build a cohesive productive team. The second is my management information system expertise to create the network system to keep us quick and efficient. In terms of personnel, I've hired over 3,500 employees and, using job accountability and training, achieved highly productive bottomline results. I utilized my computer expertise to select hardware, software, and transportation, distribution, and accounting systems to analyze and streamline costs, and put in place the most effective safeguards and systems that will maximize profits. I've always produced measurable bottomline results and feel that I would produce the same for you."

Events Planner

When interviewing for an events coordinator position with heavy computer and desktop publishing skills required, our new grad said:

"I have assisted with numerous special events during the

last two years, planning conferences, receptions, lunches, and dinners. I've been responsible for all the details, the facilities, catering and lodging arrangements, equipment and food setups, and taking care of the transportation needs, plus handling expenses and vouchers. I have learned to make any budget work, being resourceful not to exceed the budget's limits. I have had a great deal of experience comparing and selecting service contractors such as caterers and facilities.

"My computer strengths have been most beneficial to my previous employer. I have extensive IBM and Macintosh experience and easily use Pagemaker to create brochures, flyers, program schedules, invitations, and training materials. I am very quick on the Internet when needing to search or research information, or download items to enhance our materials. It is both the experience in event planning and my computer skills that would help me succeed in your position."

Engineer

When interviewing with the major automotive manufacturer for a quality-assurance engineer position, his 60 Second Sell went something like this:

"For my last employer I implemented a new quality-assurance program for seven plants over a four-year period. We received the Q-1 award for our efforts. Along the way, I've learned to effectively deal with employee resistance to quality improvements through training, selling the teamwork concepts, and utilizing a personal empowerment approach. I have evaluated 37 suppliers during on-site inspections to improve the quality of their product—parts that will ultimately become pieces of my company's final product. My five years in design engineering and my strong communication skills have aided me in my ability to work with a diverse population and solve technical problems. These are the reasons I feel I would make a valuable contribution to your company."

Summary

Both the 60 Second Sell and the 5 Point Agenda must be created for *each* interview. They may vary slightly or greatly based on what you determine to be that employer's most important needs and your most marketable abilities to meet those needs. These tools allow you to take control of the interview and get the employer to recognize the kind of abilities and contributions you will bring to the job and organization.

Your future is what you make it.

Dream BIG!

Chapter 4

Hiring Trends

Hiring practices have undergone a significant change recently. In the past, an employer would seek out an employee to "fill the job description," but the rapidly changing marketplace now requires companies to compete globally and to look for nimble employees who focus on maximizing productivity.

The most notable of these hiring trends are:

- Individuals now seek out personally rewarding work and challenges to achieve personal accomplishments.
- Employers look for future potential and a success attitude, as well as experience.
- Job seekers must now package and present the "ideal worker persona" (highly flexible and adaptable) to land the most desirable and lucrative jobs.
- Employers negotiate salary and benefits with more latitude than ever before at all job levels (most significantly, middle and upper).

In the future, workers will put more emphasis on finding personally rewarding work. Baby boomers and generation X'ers alike now value achievement accomplishments, like creating new products or programs or starting new divisions and companies, more than old standards such as titles or career ladders. It's this need for personal achievement, feeling productive and performing work that has meaning that is motivating many people when they look for new jobs.

Where People Want to Work

In recent years, new workers have flocked to fast-growing companies. The magic was no longer with the mega-large Fortune 500 companies (e.g., GM, Ford, and Exxon) but with trendsetters like Microsoft that were breaking new ground as well as offering interesting jobs and excitement in accomplishing new and cutting-edge goals. These emerging companies also offered salaries and stock options that highly rewarded the productivity of the worker. They offered a wide range of jobs and opportunities. As a result, these are highly sought after jobs, and these companies receive over 10,000 resumés each month from people hoping to work there. Sound competitive? You bet it is—and it will remain that way.

Other workers—whether new or already employed—began to look for employers whose mission they believed in as a way to find meaning in their work. Whether it was to fight for a political cause, such as the environment, or to help others overcome life's problems, such as homelessness or serious illness, they selected jobs and employers because they could make an important difference by working there. Meaningful work and helping others—not salary or stock options—were their daily incentive. Because of the work—

and the importance of the mission—these jobs are also very competitive.

Employers' Changing Needs

While workers focus on what they want from their work, global competitiveness, mergers, acquisitions, and technology are reshaping the way employers do business. Restructuring and the laying off of workers are commonplace, and yet at the same time these companies are actively recruiting new key people to help them move forward.

For example, an article in a recent issue of *Aviation Week* describing how employers such as Boeing, Raytheon, BF Goodrich, and Honeywell have changed hiring practices noted what so many employers are saying: There is often a mismatch between skills a company needs and the skills their current workers offer. The new trend is to look for people with broader-based skills, those demonstrating the ability to shift from one project to another and grow into future jobs. Hiring now takes on a more futurist look. Companies seek not only experience, but to hire people for their aptitude (what they can do) and their attitude (what they are willing to do). Most employers need productive workers that can fit into a team-based organization. The need to hire people who can grow with the company is critical whether it employs 20 people or 200,000. As a result, employers look for managers who show leadership strength, people who are "change agents," who can delegate, schedule, achieve goals, and maximize resources while also watching the bottomline. Across the United States, emerging companies, nonprofits, Fortune 500 companies, and governmental agencies are all responding to a need to have an adaptable workforce. Therefore the desire to find and hire the "ideal worker persona" is the most significant of all hiring changes.

Need to Be the Ideal Worker Persona

Older workers have been and will continue to be hard hit by layoffs. Many find it a tremendous challenge to find a new job as good as the one they lost in part because younger workers are perceived to be better fits for companies. It's not just that they are cheaper, but that they bring a more flexible skillset to the workplace. They model the desired ideal worker persona: a quick learner who is adaptable, flexible, and willing to try and succeed at new tasks. They have superior computer skills—essential for most of today's better-playing jobs. Age is NOT a barrier to developing this highly desired persona, but attitude is. Many older workers get content, or busy with their families, or distracted by serious personal problems. Yet developing this new proactive approach to performing your job is not difficult. Workers of any age can develop these traits that will increase their job security by making them more appealing to employers. Job security lies within the worker—in his talents, skills, and measurable achievements. It is your perceived potential that ensures you'll always be able to find a new job. No company offers a permanent guarantee of work anymore. Today, savvy workers always keep the door open and are on the lookout to move to a better position. Here are the keys to developing the ideal worker persona skillset:

- **Choose a field and type of work you love.** It'll be a great deal easier. Passion gives us a purpose and ignites our interest to continue to learn, and learning is the key.
- **Be a lifelong learner.** Improving your skills and diversifying them is critical to lifetime success and employment. It also makes you more

enthusiastic, and thus appealing, during a job
interview.
- **Go to work with a success attitude.** Focus
  your attitude on productivity and constantly look
  for ways to save money, save time, and improve
  the company as well as your own individual
  performance. This attitude entails being
  efficient—wasting less time socializing,
  gossiping, or doing personal things while at
  work. It also helps contribute to a congenial
  workplace where employees are able to get more
  done during the hours on the job.
- **Be flexible and adaptable.** This last component
  of the ideal worker persona means finding
  solutions, making suggestions, solving problems;
  it also means taking on new projects, tasks, or
  responsibilities. Be willing to become the worker
  the employer needs today and tomorrow rather
  than just doing the job as defined when you are
  hired.

Once you've mastered these desired traits, you will have
success at job interviews and will receive promotions because you will be seen as the ideal worker that the employer
wants to hire and keep.

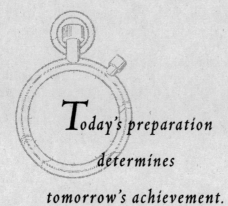

Today's preparation determines tomorrow's achievement.

Chapter 5

60-Second Answers to Tough, Tricky Questions

There are four key components to successfully answering interview questions:

- Advance preparation
- Giving short, concise, specific answers that never exceed 60 seconds
- Demonstrating ability to perform the job
- Exhibiting the ideal worker persona traits

The key to answering even the toughest questions is to think about them and prepare answers before the interview starts.

In order to help you prepare, I've answered 90 tough, tricky questions, including the typical ones you'll most likely be asked. Knowing how to answer the employer's questions is vital to your success. Your self-confidence is dependent on knowing you can effectively answer questions that demonstrate to the employer you can do his job. I'll show where to use examples that reiterate your 5 Point Agenda and where to use your 60 Second Sell.

Employers know that nervousness can cause job hunters

to babble endlessly. Demonstrate your self-confidence and retain their interest with short, effective answers. Too often job hunters answer a question, pause, get nervous, and add more information which takes away from the initial answer. Monosyllabic answers are not effective either. Strive to be concise but also complete. Short, concise answers that encourage a conversation and exchange of information is the goal.

Whenever possible, give a specific example of how you've operated in the past. Employers want assurance you'll be able to do the job. Offering explanations that include examples of how you solved a problem, saved money, or added to the bottomline are very influential. While not all skills or accomplishments can be quantified, many can, so practice sharing them. It's wise to have specific examples to point out any positive results you've achieved, whether it's reorganizing the filing system or trimming production costs through some process change. Examples can also include the results of volunteer jobs and outside activities. These are skills you have acquired and will use on the job.

Whenever possible, use descriptive words that paint a picture of how well you've performed the task in the past. Also include how willing you are to take on new tasks as needed. Your willingness to learn and be a value-added asset to the company, keeping its needs in mind, will make you a very appealing candidate.

Behavioral Interviewing and Situational Questions

Behavioral interviewing techniques are becoming very common. This style of interviewing asks you to give specific examples of positive and negative work situations. Job hunters frequently find these questions very difficult. The interviewer uses this probing style to determine how you have performed in the past. These questions often start out with "Give me an example," or "Tell me about a time," or "Describe a situation." They seek details of your past abilities and performance. Then the interviewer rates each response to determine and predict your future performance with her company. These situational questions are thought-provoking ones. The interviewer will likely take notes on each answer and continue the line of questioning looking for *specifics*: specific details, specific illustrations. Practice answering these types of questions by giving concise, detailed examples. Be sure you select examples that clearly sell those skills in the 5 Point Agenda that you have shaped to meet this employer's needs. Be concise; tell the whole story in 60 seconds or less. You're unlikely to know in advance who will use this format, so be prepared. Typically, Human Resources personnel and recruiters are the ones to use this style. More and more college students are being asked these questions, but so are managers, senior executives, professionals, staff, and everyone else in between. A human resources manager at a Fortune 500 company explained it this way: "We are so worried about lawsuits, we now instruct our managers and HR people to ask only work-related questions that ask for specific examples. Every interviewee gets the same questions, designed to evaluate their skills to perform that specific job based on the examples they give us."

Some of the following questions will have the word "Situational" at the end to tip you off to those that need you to offer concrete examples. I've included several questions you might encounter, with appropriate responses. I advise you to prepare several examples in advance to help you sail through these challenging interviews.

Answering the Questions

Review the explanations and answers below, then choose
your own words and formulate your answers to potential
questions. The result: You'll be prepared to handle any
question concisely, getting your point across in 60 seconds
or less.

1. *"Why did you leave your last job?"*
I guarantee that you'll get asked this question, so having
an appropriate, acceptable answer is a must. Good reasons
to depart include wanting more challenge or growth opportunities, relocation, layoffs, or reorganization or downsizing
which affected your duties. A typical answer might be, "The
company went through a downsizing; that's why I'm available." Another answer might be, "My current employer is
small and I've gone as far as I can with their organization.
I'm looking for a challenge that will really use my abilities
and strengths to continue to grow and make a contribution." A different response could be, "We've just relocated
to this area to be near our family, and that's why I'm available."

2. *"Tell me about your proudest accomplishments."*
Review your 60 Second Sell and 5 Point Agenda. Think
about what you're trying to stress, and then write down
three big work-related accomplishments that demonstrate
your ability to do the employer's job. Employment, community, or association work can often be examined to find just
the right example to make your point. Avoid noting personal achievements such as "I lost 75 pounds" or "I won the
5K race." Better to illustrate work accomplishments, citing
specific examples, such as, "I am proud of the newsletter I
started as a part of our fundraising efforts. It has helped in-

crease donations by 20% and we've had a great deal of positive feedback on it."

3. *"Describe your ideal supervisor."*

This is really saying, "Can you work with me?" Frame your answer accordingly. Point out the type of management style that allows you to be the most productive on the job.

4. *"Describe the worst supervisor you've ever had."* *(Situational)*

As much as you want to criticize an old boss and point out that person's faults, I suggest you reconsider. Many employers have told me this will reflect negatively on you if you do. Instead try this: "One boss didn't give me very much feedback. In fact, I only heard from him when there was a problem. Months might go by without any kind of feedback or idea of what he was thinking. Although I don't like to have someone standing over my shoulder, I do like to have input, exchange ideas, and get a feel that my work is in line with my boss's and the company's goals. Open communication, I guess, is what was lacking. I think that's really important to have between me and a supervisor." This answer demonstrates a positive response on how teamwork is important in achieving the employer's goals.

In some positions, though, workers need to take on a great deal of autonomy. This is a growing trend. In this case, you might frame your answer this way: "I'm good at my job and for two years I had a boss who gave us a great deal of autonomy. I flourished, meeting all the goals and at times exceeding them. My boss moved on, and the current supervisor is a micromanager. This is harder for me and most of the other employees to adjust to. I think having clear goals and then allowing me to proceed on my own is how I'm most productive."

5. *"What features of your previous job did you like?"*
   (Situational)

When you talk about things that you like, relate them to the job you're going to do for this potential employer. Talk specifically about things that she's going to have you do in this job, such as facilitate training sessions, run an Excel program, handle the budget, or organize a project from start to finish.

6. *"What features of your last job did you dislike?"*
   (Situational)

This is a tricky one. Be sure you point out something that won't affect your ability to do this employer's job. When you select an example, use information you know about the new job, such as the fact that all this company's publications are printed out of house. At your old job, everything was done in-house. So you might answer with, "One of the things I really disliked was the length of time needed to complete printing projects. We did things in-house; many times everything was backed up several weeks. I found it frustrating to need seven weeks to complete a project that we could have turned around at a commercial printing place within five days. I felt the process was not very productive or effective."

7. *"What is your greatest weakness?"*

I always tell managers attending my seminar on hiring to ask this question because many times the job candidate gives them evidence of how they can*not* do the job. Recently at a seminar with senior executives, a CFO related this story: "I was hiring for a staff accountant position. When I asked the guy to tell me his weaknesses he said, 'Well, sometimes I get the 3 and the 8 mixed up, but it all seems to come out okay in the end.' The 3 and the 8—we are in finance!" he exclaimed, emphasizing his exasperation with this confession. I repeat this example because this question causes many people to make a serious error, as this applicant did.

If you think about this in advance and you have a written-out answer, it's really not that tough a question. I recommend that you pick something that has nothing to do with your ability to accomplish the job. An answer that I always used was, "Well, I'm not very mechanical, so when the copy machine breaks down, you better not call me." Ha, ha, ha, joke, joke, joke. A little humor in the interview is definitely okay. And often we would go on to the next question. But if the interviewer came back and said, "No, now really, what is your greatest weakness?" I might say, "Well you know, sometimes when I'm working on a project I just get so absorbed, I forget to look at the time. Before you know, the time to leave has long gone by and I'm still there. I guess that's a weakness. I guess I should realize that you should be able to leave right at five. But when I'm working on a project and I'm being creative, and things are rolling, I just stay on until I can get it done." Here a weakness is turned into a positive, appealing trait. Try to choose something that's not going to hurt your chances of getting hired. A better answer for our accountant might have been to say, "I have excellent computer user skills. I know Excel inside and out, but I am pretty weak at actual programming and would need more training if I were to write your software programs." No one's asking him to rewrite software, and his answer actually reinforces his major selling point—his computer skills. With advance thought you can choose something similar that will have no negative impact on the hiring decision.

8. *"What are your strengths?"*

You respond with your 60 Second Sell. Tailor it to the particular needs of this job.

9. *"Describe a time when you were criticized for poor
    performance." (Situational)*

This question is a minefield. You must use a specific incident, yet carefully choose an example that demonstrates
what you did to correct the situation. Select an example such
as poor public speaking skills, which allows you to continue
on to say that you enrolled in a class and after several
months you are now quite proficient. This demonstrates
your ability to take constructive criticism and improve.
Avoid answers that deal with late arrivals, absenteeism, or
interpersonal conflicts, as these often send red-flag warnings
to an employer about your dependability and ability to fit
into an organization.

10. *"I'm a little worried about your lack of . . ."*

If the employer is unaware of your experience, such as
computer skills, then it's easy to give an answer using an example. "At my old company, I was responsible for a lot of
the data entry. I used a mainframe with customized software. I have a natural aptitude for computers and would be
willing to spend lunch hours and some evenings on my own
time learning your software so I can come up to speed
quickly."

If the employer is concerned about a skill you do lack
but are eager to learn, try, "I appreciate your honesty. I have
excellent customer services skills, but you are right, I have
not been a salesperson. I do know the keys to success are
building good client relationships, persistence, using good
time management skills, being good at follow-up, and learning the trade. I have read numerous books on selling and understand the process. I intend to take seminars at my own
expense to learn everything I can about selling. I am a hard
worker, and I let rejection roll off my back. My goals include
landing a sales job and then becoming one of the top sales-
people in my company. I'm determined to succeed."

11. *"You have a lot of experience. Why would you want this job?"*

The employer fears you are overqualified and will get bored and want to leave his job quickly if he hires you. Or he may suspect that you are simply burned-out and looking for an easy job now and won't be productive. You have anticipated this question. Do not oversell your abilities. Do not show that you are desperate, that you'll take *any* job. Stress why this job fits for you now. Talk about life changes, need for more structure, desire to make a long-term contribution. You can say that you seek to spend more time with your family and therefore want a job with less travel or overtime demands. Be careful not to say you want an easy, no-stress job, causing the employer to doubt whether you would do all the work that needs to be done.

12. *"Describe a difficult coworker you've had to deal with." (Situational)*

Careful, we are looking for turf wars, troublesome employees, and any red flags you care to raise. Try to show a misunderstanding and your efforts to correctly resolve it. "I dealt with the engineering manager, who is often blunt and can hurt others' feelings. He was always sharp with my assistant and one day was particularly so over a report he needed. As she was greatly upset, I decided to discuss what was becoming a problem. I approached it from his perspective, that of a visual, analytical thinker. I asked him to write me when requesting reports and to state the day and time he needed them so that I could assure him he'd get them on time. I then mentioned that my assistant was a competent, but sensitive, person, and that yesterday he had upset her and that I would appreciate his help in dealing with her. I proceeded to brainstorm with him on ways we could all improve to work together."

Here you've pointed out a problem and the solution of

working together and asking for input. Open-minded, but also responding to your staff's needs. Select an example that demonstrates both.

13. *"Describe how you work under pressure, deadlines, etc." (Situational)*

The interviewer is interested in your time management skills and workload organization. Try: "I try to plan out all major projects in a reverse time line. I start with the deadline and work backward to set divisional deadlines for the pieces of the project. I work well under pressure. I have always made deadlines in the past. I use time management and planning grids, to-do lists, project scheduling, and spreadsheets. I even plan for the inevitable snag or two that may come up. These tools help me to best utilize my time and to avoid becoming frantic and overloaded as the last hours of a deadline draw near."

14. *"What do you know about our company?"*

The temptation here is to spend an hour regurgitating all the market research you've done on the company. Better to sum it all up in what they need, like this: "That I could be a strong contributor. I know you need someone who can . . . ," and then go into your 60 Second Sell.

15. *"What two or three things are most important to you in your job?"*

Select two or three points from your 5 Point Agenda and frame your answer to say, "It's important that I use my skills to be a productive contributor to my company. I believe when I'm using organizational and planning skills, I'm working at my best. That's important to me." Be sure to select two or three items essential to doing the employer's job successfully.

16. *"Why did you change jobs so frequently?"*

Job-hopping has become more common as we have become a more mobile society and with all the downsizing and failed businesses. Dual-career families are often relocating, with one spouse's job history showing numerous changes. Job-hopping is something that really concerns an employer, who knows it takes months for people to learn a job. She worries that you'll just be trained, and then take off. Often the truth works best. If you have moved a lot, try, "My husband's position required us to move quite often. His last promotion here guaranteed that we would remain in the area permanently. I'm eager to get my career on track and bring long-term contributions to my employer. On the various jobs, I have developed excellent program management skills; I know numerous software programs and quickly become a productive worker."

Or if the job changes came from obtaining better positions: "Each position allowed me to learn new skills, and every job was on a promotional path. Most have been with very small companies, where leaving was the only option for advancement. I'm now looking for an organization where I can stay and make a long-term contribution."

17. *"What do you think of your previous boss?"*

If you loved your boss, this is an easy one. If you found your boss difficult to work with, be careful when phrasing your answer. Negative comments send up a red flag of a problem employee. Resist the urge to bad-mouth your boss. Try, "My boss had extensive experience in the field and I learned a lot working under her," or "My boss had an open-door policy and was very approachable. I found this to be an asset in our working relationship."

18. *"This is a very high pressured job. Do you think
    you're up to it?"*

The only way to prove you can handle pressure is to give
an example. Applicants for sales, customer service, operations, and top management positions often get this question. Create an example like this: "Cabinet sales is a
high-pressure business. Our margins are tight and we constantly need new business. Last year we opened a new terri-
tory, and the heat was on for us to produce. I met with my
sales team and we established new goals. I let them pick the
reward structure that motivated them. Most chose a paid vacation, not higher commissions. So every week I sent a note
with a picture of their goal—Hawaii scenes, a freshly
painted house, dollar bills—to keep up the momentum. It
worked, and the entire department was rewarded for sur-
passing corporate's goals."

19. *"Why do you want to leave your present job?"*

Companies want to hear that you seek more challenge,
more advancement, a promotion, more financial reward.
You can also leave to shorten your commute or because your
company is unstable. Try, "I have learned so much working
for my current company, but there are no promotional opportunities. I enjoy challenges and learning new skills as
well as improving my old ones. Therefore, I seek a new position at this time." Or "I noticed that your company had an
opening. I've been very happy at my present position, but
the option to move to a good company, such as yours, and
only have a 10-minute commute is very appealing. Right
now I commute 45 minutes to an hour each way." Or, for a
small company, try, "I've gained a lot of experience at my
other positions. But now I want an opportunity for more responsibility, to have greater impact on the end results. Your
company will really allow me to see the fruits of my labor,
and that is important to me."

20. *"Do you mind routine work?"*

The key here is to recognize that routine work is the job. Your answer should be, "I enjoy structure; it allows me to be efficient in doing the tasks correctly."

21. *"Have you ever been asked to resign?"*

The answer to this question is "no." You were either fired or laid off, or you chose to quit. You may have been presented with the option of leaving, but you still chose to leave. Too many lawsuits have been initiated over this issue. Your former employer would not likely admit to forcing you out. Therefore, honestly say "no."

22. *"Tell me about one of your failures." (Situational)*

This is a very tricky question. I suggest you answer by giving an example of a setback or a learning experience and show what you did to improve. "I decided that our company would benefit by having a lunchtime brown-bag training program. I lined up some speakers, scheduled the room, and sent out a notice. Four people showed, out of over 800. The next event drew three people. I had failed, but I couldn't understand why. I asked numerous employees, and kept hearing that the topics *were* of interest. Most wanted to know what they'd learn and wanted a relaxed, fun setting. I asked a friend in marketing, who suggested using a snappy title for the program and each seminar. Changing the copy and using graphics did the trick. During a recent company survey, the luncheon program was rated as an important benefit and drew 75 to 80 employees per meeting. You see, I believe there aren't failures, only learning experiences, which is what I experienced here."

23. *"We work a lot of late nights here. Is that going to cause any trouble at home?"*

"I am able and willing to work whatever hours you need me. I expected that with this position evenings would be necessary, as they were in my previous position." Reassure the employer that you will work the hours he needs. Your reliability and dependability is what he is questioning.

24. *"You have too much experience for this job. Why would you want it?"*

Employers are reluctant to hire a person who is over-qualified because they think the person is unlikely to be happy, stay long, or be seriously interested just in doing the job hired for. They do not want someone who is burned-out and sees their job as an easy paycheck. Often you can be threatening to the interviewer, especially if you are truly suited for the interviewer's job. Examine why you want the position. "I need a job" is not a response that will endear you to an interviewer. You must use your acting skills to convince her why a demotion is a good option. Try: "My current position as controller requires 10 nights of travel per month. This has become an increasingly difficult sacrifice for my family. I have decided to seek an accounting position that allows me to focus on my strengths—taxes, audits, and computer integration—but that allows me to go home each evening. The subsidiary I work for is typical of similar companies in our industry—the controller position requires a lot of out-of-town travel to do the job, which I no longer want to do. I believe the extensive financial skills I would bring would benefit your organization in a positive way. I see this as a win/win situation for both of us." Create a reasonable explanation. Showing desperation and being willing to take any job often makes the interviewer disqualify you. The company needs that job done and you must show you can do it, but also that you *want* to do it.

25. *"You've been with the same company for so many years, how will you cope with a new one?"*

The interviewer is concerned that you'll be slow to adapt and change. Dispel that. "I have always been flexible and adaptable in taking on new tasks. I pride myself on being a constant learner. You'd benefit from my . . ." Use your 60 Second Sell to point out the experience you'd bring.

26. *"What was it about your last job that bothered you the most?" (Situational)*

Here the interviewer is looking for incompatibles: things you dislike that are aspects of his company's job. The best way to answer this is to select something that is either neutral or that would be a benefit. For example, "At my old company we had a very slow computer and an MS Office program that was two versions old. It took a lot of extra time and had fewer capabilities than the newest additions. I found it bothersome, but my old company didn't have the funds to update their equipment. As the editor of my association's newsletter, I used top-of-the-line equipment like you have here and it made for a higher-quality, faster-produced product. I'd look forward to using your equipment each day."

27. *"What motivates you?"*

"Using my strengths and abilities to be a highly productive employee. I take pride in my work and am most motivated when I use my _____ skills." Fill in that blank, naming the skills in your 5 Point Agenda.

28. *"How creative a problem solver are you?"*

This question is very tricky in that you aren't sure what the employer is getting at. You also want to know if there are big problems that not enough funds and resources are available to fix. Therefore, I recommend you answer with a question to clarify what's being asked. Try: "In the past, I've been a resourceful problem solver. Could you be more specific about the types of problems I'll need to solve here? Then I can give you examples of what I've done in the past." Be sure to get a good answer at some point in the hiring process about the company's stability and the depth of the problems the company and your department face.

29. "Describe a large mistake you made at your last job." (Situational)

Select an example that demonstrates a learning experience and shows how you corrected the mistake. You might try something like: "I was under very tight deadlines and we had a large volume of work to get done. I only glanced at some important letters my assistant had done and signed the letters. Unfortunately, the meeting time and location were incorrect. It was embarrassing and required time I didn't have to call the 20 individuals and correct the error, but that's what I did. I smoothed it over, but my boss noticed and spoke to me about it. I sat down with my assistant and calmly discussed how we could prevent these errors in the future. Together we decided that we would read the information to each other and triple-check to verify dates, times, and locations. We decided to try to replan our work time to be less pushed at the last minute to catch the day's mail. I volunteered to bring the mail to the post office so we wouldn't have to rush to get everything done before our 1:00 mail pickup." Here you've stressed teamwork, gaining staff cooperation, and problem solving. To err is human, but it is the *solutions* that you employ to fix or eliminate errors that matter to an employer.

30. "How would you describe your ideal job?"

Explain that the perfect job is one that uses your talents and allows you to be most productive. Mention several of your strengths from your 5 Point Agenda. The tendency for most job hunters is to get into elaborate discussions here about what they want—salary, benefits, work environment—and not focus on doing the employer's job. Save the salary and benefits discussions until after he makes the offer. For now, you need to still convince him you're the right one for the job. This is a great opportunity to stress that you enjoy learning new things, are adaptable, and are willing to take on new tasks as needed. Reiterating that you possess the traits of the ideal worker persona is always a plus.

31. *"How do you think your present/last boss would describe you?" (Situational)*

Whether you and your boss like each other is not the issue. Simply fall back on your 5 Point Agenda and describe your work. Mention three or four points that your boss would note that are important to doing this employer's job. Give an example of some task or project you've been praised for. If you plan to use your boss as a reference, it makes a very strong statement if you end by saying: "My boss will be happy to verify this; feel free to call her."

32. *"How would you rate yourself as a leader? A supervisor? An employee?"*

Analytical individuals often rate themselves low because they look to improve everything, including themselves, and that is not a good approach here. Start with the employee part first. You could say, "I'm a highly regarded employee because I'm productive and good at what I do." If you are a supervisor and manager, continue on to say, "I treat everyone fairly, and that allows me to have a good working relationship with my staff. I'm approachable, but I also hold each person accountable for doing his job well and achieving the department's goals. In the past, my department has always been recognized for its productivity under my leadership." You can say this even if you've won no awards. All departments have goals, and if you achieve yours then it signifies that you are in sync with the company's demands.

33. *"You've worked for yourself now for a while, so why do you want to work for our company?"*

The truth is that self-employment is hard work. It takes endless hours, excellent business operation knowledge, capital, marketing skills, and perseverance to survive. Four out of five small businesses fail. The employer doesn't want an employee who is burned-out and wants an easy paycheck. And life changes—a divorce, an ill spouse—often create the need for a steady income and company benefits. These are usually the real reasons. Think through the answer and then respond honestly. "I really am at my best training employees. I get outstanding evaluations and work hard to create an effective learning environment. I found that as a consultant at least 40% of my time was spent on marketing and business development. I failed to make follow-up calls because I would rather rework and improve my curriculum. I found I disliked 'selling,' so I made a decision to seek employment. The job I really want is to spend all my time training others. I enjoy working with clients to determine their needs and then offer them a good seminar or training session to help employees improve on the job. Your company's position allows me to use my strengths as a trainer and focus on just that—training." It's important to calm any fears that the employer may have about how difficult you might be to manage. Showing you work well with others is also a key point to stress.

34. *"Give me an example of a time you had to deal with criticism from your boss."* *(Situational)*

No one likes to be criticized. The truth is, most of us get a little hurt, maybe angry, definitely defensive. To answer this question, it is best to point out an idea that was criticized, or work that you corrected and improved. Be careful—your answer can cause the interviewer to question your ability to do their job. You could give an example such as: "I remember a time when I was a rather new employee in a meeting of all the store department managers. We discussed increasing the company's sales among our younger customers. My idea was to advertise in a certain magazine. I was heavily criticized by two other department heads. I kept cool and restated my reasons, which were clear to me but' not to them. After the meeting, I wrote out the idea and noted some of our own market research that supported my suggestion. I also sent it along to the sales manager. Months passed, and a competitor used my idea as part of their advertising campaign, with good success. My boss and the sales manager both reevaluated my input then, and I believe I gained more respect from the department heads for my ideas after that."

If you select an example about your work's needing improvement, demonstrate the steps you took to correct the situation. "I gave a presentation to our executive group. I was nervous and not prepared for all the questions they asked, nor was I very good at ad-libbing when my Power Point program crashed. My boss pointed out several weak points to me later. His feedback was hard to take at the time, but I followed up on his suggestions. I worked on my presentation style—I took a class and even had myself videotaped. My boss's feedback was important in helping me improve my job performance, and recently he commented on how polished and professional I am as a public speaker."

35. *"What's the most difficult challenge you've faced in your life?" (Situational)*

You will need to discuss a specific example that demonstrates how tough the situation was and how you handled it. I often recommend you stick to work-related situations.

Avoid discussing coworker problems unless you can show how you changed your approach or attitude to improve the working relationship. Personal tragedies, broken relationships, and sick family members are usually our most difficult challenges in life, but discussing them in an interview can cause extreme emotional reactions within you. This could create a problem for you in handling the rest of the interview with the employer, or raise doubts about your emotional stability and dependability on the job. It's best to stay away from these personal subjects. If you have ever had to fire someone, then use that experience. Everyone finds it difficult to take away a person's livelihood. State how you tried to improve the worker's performance, carefully considered the decision, and then, with professionalism, terminated the employee.

36. *"What are you doing now to improve yourself?"*

Employers value employees who believe in lifelong learning. It is best to note that you are taking a course or reading a book to gain or improve a skill. You could say, "I joined Toastmasters three months ago to work on perfecting my public speaking skills," or "I presently am going to college at night to pursue a degree in business." Another option is to say, "I enjoy doing research on the Internet and spend free time downloading graphics and articles we can use in our office."

37. *"How would you influence someone to accept your ideas?"*

The interviewer is interested in evaluating the depth of your communication skills and your ability to persuade others. Try: "I've learned that it is important to offer an idea using the right framework. It is important to look at who is the person or persons evaluating the idea and then determining the best approach that will appeal to them. I always have a rationale for why and how the idea will work. I try to think through the details beforehand. I'm open-minded about the feedback my idea gets and look for ways to improve it or implement it so it will work well." Another approach might be: "In sales, the key is always stress the benefits to the person I'm talking to. That's exactly what I try to do."

38. *"Could you explain in detail your experience with computer software programs?" (Situational)*

Be very specific in answering this question, but first ask what the company is using. Computer skills are right at the top of employer survey lists as the number one skill they seek from employees. You might say, "Are you on a network system?" If the interviewer says yes, then go on, "Do you use Microsoft Office?" If so, continue with, "That's what we have now. I work mostly with two programs, Word and Excel. I'm a very advanced user on Word. I can do mail merges, and create sophisticated charts and graphics. I use Word every day. On Excel I can create spreadsheets and formulas easily." This shows you're a high-level user. If you know the company has different software, you might continue to say, "I believe that software is very similar to Excel. I know all the concepts and feel it wouldn't take much time to become proficient in it. I would certainly be willing to put in some of my own time to speed up the learning process."

39. *"Tell me about something your boss did that you disliked." (Situational)*

It's best not to criticize your boss, though noting something like, "He smoked," if you are certain the interviewer does not, is okay. If not, say, "I never really view a work relationship in those terms. We have a job to do and we all work together to do it well."

40. "How do you organize and plan for major projects?" (Situational)

Stress in-depth planning and tracking, plus your efficient time management. "Currently, I use timelines, to-do lists, responsibility charts, staff progress meetings, problem-solving sessions, and goal setting, and a sophisticated project manager software system."

41. "What was the last book you read?"

Often this is a question to see what you read off the job. A common mistake is to select a current hot business book and drop that title. More often than not, the next questions will lead to an extensive discussion of that book's principles and theories and a defense of your opinions. So don't try to fake it to impress the interviewer—state a book you know well enough that you can talk about the plot or content. This isn't a critical question, so don't get too concerned if you answer with a novel and not a job or business book.

42. "Tell us about a personal goal that you still want to achieve."

Share a goal that would increase your value as a worker. Cite a new skill—supervisor training, hiring experience, a new computer program—that, once learned, increases your value to the employer. A specialized degree or training courses you want to complete can also be a good choice.

43. "Describe to me your typical workday." (Situational)

Here the interviewer wants to know specifics to confirm you have handled most of their responsibilities before. Be sure to cover their most important duties in your answer, emphasizing the points in your 5 Point Agenda. Offer to give more specific details if he'd like, but try not to overwhelm him with a verbose and lengthy reply.

44. *"Have you ever had any problems with poor attendance?" (Situational)*

If the answer is no, say, "No, I haven't." This can easily be verified with references. If you have had a problem, then try to analyze what the problem was and offer a solution. Typical daycare issues could be covered by saying, "When I was at ABC, my salary was lower than average, which created difficulties in finding appropriate daycare. I often missed work when my child was sick because I could not afford a private sitter. I discussed this problem with my boss and my friends. I then decided that the situation wasn't fair to anyone. I asked my boss for a raise based on the quality of my work, which was high and well regarded. He explained that the company had no budgets for raises. I then decided to look for a new job. Since I've been at X Company, I've never missed a day. I have a good daycare situation that will take a sick child. I learned a lot about resourcefulness, and my value as a worker. I put 110% into my job, and I know my current boss will attest to my productivity levels and good attendance."

If illness was the reason, you might say, "Once I was dealing with a personal illness and was absent often over several weeks. It was completely resolved within three months and I'm quite healthy now and my most recent attendance has been excellent." In this question, the employer just wants assurances that your reliability won't be a problem.

45. *"Have you ever been responsible for managing financial budgets or department expenses?" (Situational)*

If the answer is yes, be specific. "Yes, I oversee my department's budget and approve all purchase orders and expenses. My budget is $200,000 annually and requires me to be resourceful and cautious in spending my department's funds." It is always good to add that you are cautious about spending someone else's money.

46. *"What are the three most important responsibilities in your present job?" (Situational)*

Simply discuss the three areas that will be the most important to that employer in doing her job. Select them from your 5 Point Agenda.

47. *"Tell me about an unpopular decision you had to make." (Situational)*

Positions of responsibility often require making hard choices. Select a time when you chose the lesser of two evils or when you provided solid explanations for a cost-cutting measure. You could say, "Our company was downsizing and we had to trim our labor costs. As the department manager, I selected dropping benefits and not terminating our employees. I sat down with the department's staff, stated the problem, and asked for their input. As a group, they all wanted to fire the most recently hired. Unfortunately, these new jobs were critical to the company's future. I decided to eliminate all insurance benefits (life, dental, disability, and retirement) but retain the medical coverage with a small co-payment. Many of our longer-term staff complained. I listened to them, but did what I felt served the company and department best."

If you ever had to fire a well-liked person, you might say, "I had a very popular employee work for me who was ineffective and had low performance on her job. She was very friendly, but not able to learn the computer skills we needed. I elected to fire her. One person complained all the way up to the CEO. They often admitted her work was inferior, but said she was such a nice person that I should not have fired her. Although my boss agreed with my choice, I took the heat and then carefully hired a new person who had the necessary skills. I purposely hired someone who would blend well with our other staff. In the end, it was the best thing for the department though personally rather difficult for me."

48. *"Give me an example of when it was necessary to reach a goal within a very short period of time and what you did to achieve it." (Situational)*

Select an example that demonstrates resourcefulness, adaptability, and pitching in wherever necessary. For example: "The marketing department needed some data to produce a new brochure and we had three weeks to research it, design it, and write the new copy. Two days after we got the assignment, the sales department had secured a huge presentation to our most sought after client. They needed the brochure printed in seven days. Top priority. I reorganized my schedule and the graphic designer's. We forwarded calls to voice mail and stayed late, and within two days produced the copy and design needed to get the job done. The sales department made the pitch two days early, and we landed a very big account as a result. I can't say it was the brochure that did it. I think it was the desire to win, to reach the goal, that inner motivation of being part of the team. We all worked very hard to get the results we wanted."

49. *"Do you consider yourself successful?"*

Of course you do. So answer, "Yes, I do and I feel that my employer benefits because I always give 110% to my job, doing the very best I can each day."

50. *"What would you do with an individual who is very angry and complaining to you?" (Situational)*

Think about what you do when faced with an angry person. Most angry people want someone to *listen* to their rage and *solve* their complaint. Often, just listening helps. Appropriate referrals or action steps to solve the problem might work also. Screaming or foul language might require you to ask the person to calm down; and when he can more calmly explain the problem, you'll work on the solution. Your response to this question might be: "Very angry, screaming people require a time-out, a cooling-off period. I express this by telling them I can only listen if they are calm and want my help in finding a solution. I have found that listening often dissipates the anger. They want their problem fixed or solved. I know that dissatisfied customers often do a lot of damage, repeating their troubles to countless others. I do my best to find a workable solution that our organization can deal with and that will satisfy the customer."

51. *"Tell me about a time when your work performance was low." (Situational)*

Every job is affected by tragedies that happen in people's personal lives, or by a work environment that threatens layoffs and causes job insecurity. Select an example that deals with a short-lived personal crisis and show your efforts to deal with the issue to counteract your low performance. "I received some tragic news one morning that my brother was critically injured in a car crash. The workload was enormous and yet I could not really make the decisions necessary to run my department. I went to my boss and asked to reassign some of my major responsibilities, as I might need to fly across the country to be with my family. I told my staff my problem and asked for their help. My performance was below par that week. I did leave the next week to attend the funeral. Upon my return, I took the time to write each staff person a note of thanks for all they did during this difficult time. I think we all became a stronger team, though, as a result." This is a good example because you took responsibility to delegate your work and the situation was short-lived. I suggest you avoid an answer such as this: "I was going through a divorce and my work really suffered." Employers are not as sympathetic to long-term poor performance.

52. "Describe a time that you dealt with a stressful work situation." (Situational)

"I remember a time when we were short staffed over several weeks. I had been working a lot of overtime and so had my staff. One employee called in sick and we had a 5:00 P.M. deadline to make that day. It would not be possible to extend. I called the three remaining staff in and told them the situation. I asked everyone how we could finish this today. They offered good ideas, and I had lunch delivered and told everyone that if we finished today everyone could come in at noon tomorrow. It was high pressure when everyone was running on low energy, but we did it. I also went to my boss the next day to discuss how we might readjust the workload while we were minus two people." This answer demonstrates teamwork, extra efforts, and good problem-solving skills.

53. "Describe a time when you reprimanded an employee for poor performance." (Situational)

Show how you have given clear direction and training to enable others to improve at their job. "I was assigned a new administrative assistant, and she repeatedly made mistakes typing correspondence for me. If she had carefully proofread the letters, she would surely have corrected these errors. I sat down with her and brought one letter noting all my corrections. I nicely told her that I was finding too many errors in the letters and asked if she proofed each letter before she gave it to me. She said no because she felt I wanted them quickly and I always seemed to make changes anyway. I told her that I expected her to proof each letter and make all corrections before she gave them to me. I thought this would save time and that it was very important that our correspondence be perfect before we mailed it out. Since most of the work was highly technical, I suggested she take a class on proofreading and editing. As a result her performance improved."

54. "Describe a time when you felt you made a poor decision." (Situational)

This is a very tricky question. Try to select an example where your boss admitted to you that she made a mistake too. You might say: "A few years ago, I remember my boss asked me to do a presentation to our board of directors in her absence. I worked on the material, and asked my boss to let me run through the whole thing before the meeting. The day before I was to do that, my boss got tied up, so I never got her input on my research and data. I decided to just do the handouts and was embarrassed at the meeting when my figures and marketing data where heavily questioned. I got intimidated and nervous and stumbled through their questions. I made a poor choice not getting others' input when my boss was unable to assist me. She did apologize to me later and took some responsibility for not making time to help me before the meeting. I learned a valuable lesson about teamwork that day, one that has helped me become a better supervisor."

55. "Describe the environment that motivates your productivity." (Situational)

This question often has you reveal some important clues to your true work style. Try: "I find that I am most productive in an organization that expects me to do a good job, rewards me well, and has the needed resources to accomplish the goals. If you check with my references you'll find that I am a self-starter, happy when there are volumes of work to complete, and that I can be counted on to get it done right and on time." You might then ask: "How much autonomy will I have in this job?" Then you can learn how this job might suit your needs. Be sure to comment on any specifics that the interviewer replies with.

56. *"Can we check with your current employer?"*

This question often makes job hunters very nervous because their employer doesn't know they are looking for a job. To say no, try this: "My current employer is not aware I am looking for a new position, and contacting him could jeopardize the job I have. I have the names of three references here who are very familiar with my work that you can call." If you can show copies of excellent past performance appraisals, do so, but only if they are very good.

In large companies you may have someone who can be a reference besides your immediate boss, so try this approach: "My immediate boss is unaware that I am looking for a more challenging position, and I'd prefer he not be called. I do work with the controller daily as part of my duties, and you could contact her. I've put her name and number first on my reference list. The other two people have worked with me in the past in supervisory roles. I am sure they can answer any questions you have."

57. *"Describe your management style in dealing with staff and coworkers." (Situational)*

The more you know about the employer, the easier it will be to frame your answer to demonstrate your competent leadership capabilities. Your research should direct how you answer this question. Some positions require a firm approach, some demand decisive decision making; other companies like the micromanager approach, while still others prefer an open, approachable style. Dictatorial styles are passé, but there are still employers that expect that from their managers. Analyze your style and that of the company, then create your answer. You could say "In my mind, being a firm credit manager that enforces the company's rules is important. I expect my staff and I will do that. I hold each person accountable for doing his or her job and enforcing company policies. I'm a reasonable person when negotiation is required to aid clients in the process of paying their bills. I'll listen to the coworkers', staff's, and clients' needs and will change policies that become outdated or ineffective. In credit, we hear a lot of stories. I teach my staff that people will lie, and that our job is to collect the money owed the company. Using professionalism and legal guidelines, we all do just that." Another way to answer this is to offer some evidence, like past performance reviews or commendations for your management style. You might say: "I would say I bring intelligent leadership to each and every position. This coupled with my energy and enthusiasm makes me an effective manager. I've been trained in TQM (total quality management) and use it to a degree, but I've also found having a vision, articulating that vision, and recognizing and rewarding your people as they strive to realize that vision get results. In my performance evaluation, my current boss has stated that I am a superbly effective leader. Here is a copy of the review. As you can see, he said, 'Bob is dynamic, brimming with enthusiasm, and extremely perceptive. Even more importantly, he gets results with people. He has a vision, sets clear goals, and brings out the best in people with his indefatigable humor and excellent communication skills. He is one of the most capable and dedicated managers in this company.' You should call him to get a better view of how I perform on the job." Then offer the person's phone number or email address.

58. *"What would you find difficult from what you understand about this job?"*

The interviewer is looking for you to expound upon some area of weakness you have. Perhaps you've heard something that makes *you* wonder about your performance ability. In that case, ask a question such as, "I need to know more about how you use your process assessments and how that software is used in the job." Or "Could you tell me more about how large your budget is, and the resources and staff available assigned to this project first?" Quantify the employer's needs and situation, and then answer. When citing a potential problem, explain that you learn quickly and that whatever appears to be a problem will easily be solved.

If this job seems to be in line with your abilities, just start with, "I don't see any difficulties and feel I'll quickly adjust to your systems . . . ," and then continue with your 60 Second Sell.

59. *"What makes you qualified?"*
Using your 60 Second Sell will serve you best in responding to this one.

60. *"How do you handle stress?"*
Most jobs have some stress or pressure involved, and this question asks how you would respond to that stress. Be forewarned that if you bring up a specific stressful situation at work you will be asked all the details of why it happened, who contributed, and what you did and didn't do; also, you might possibly raise doubts about your effectiveness in handling the work without creating stressful environments for yourself and others. Be sure to prepare for this question in advance to prevent getting into hot water with a poor example. A good response could be: "Often stress results from inadequate time management and then feeling panicked at the end to get the job done and meet a deadline. I try to plan ahead and work efficiently to avoid last-minute pressure-cooker situations. There are times, though, when unforeseen circumstances create a stressful situation. Whenever that happens to me, I draw on my previous experience, ex-

amining what I have done in the past that has worked to help me decide how to effectively handle this present situation. The fact that I exercise three or four times a week also helps. I find it reduces my stress and increases my energy and ability to think clearly and perform better at my job."

61. "What was the most frustrating thing in your current (or last) position?" (Situational)

Again, the interviewer is looking for incompatibility with the company's job. Be sure to cite something that will not be a negative influence and hurt your chances to get hired. For example, "I hate dealing with angry patients" is a poor answer for a doctor's office nurse. A better response would be: "At my current office, our front-desk staff makes numerous errors in regard to scheduling patients and not delivering messages. I then get calls from frantic patients upset that I never returned their calls. I've suggested I get a voice mail extension to have calls transferred to me, and my doctor has agreed, but it's been three months and it hasn't happened. I believe in providing the highest quality of care possible and am glad to hear you have a good phone system in place here. I become frustrated if we don't try to offer patients the best possible quality of care, care that is sensitive to their needs, especially when they are very sick and in pain."

62. "What do you find most challenging in working with customers (clients) or coworkers?" (Situational)

Interpersonal skills and adaptability are the key points the interviewer is questioning. You might say, "I enjoy working with others. I excel at satisfying customers and solving problems. For example, . . ." Then go on to discuss a specific aspect of a past job where you dealt with customers. A retail store department manager once said, "I remember an incident a few weeks back, when a customer came in complaining that her new red satin pajamas had bled into her expensive sheets, which she had also brought in. I asked her about the cost of the sheets, and they were $250. I refunded her money on the pajamas and apologized about the sheets, giving her the name of our risk management specialist. I told her we'd call her in 24 hours about the sheets and gave her my card. I called four hours later, after I tested other pajamas we were selling and found that they did rub off just as the customer had said. I pulled the items, and we immediately sent the customer a check for $250 with our apologies. This solved the problem, and pulling the product and notifying other stores eliminated a potential catastrophe for them also." This answer outlines the problem and the solution and results. Always strive to tell your stories this way.

63. *"Name the one work characteristic that you'll bring to this job that makes you successful."*

The answer is to select the most important skill in your 5 Point Agenda and state that. Be sure you answer the question—the interviewer asked for one skill, so select and state just one. It shows you are a careful listener.

Firings/Layoffs/Work Gaps/Reentry

64. *"Were you fired from your last job or why did you leave your last job?"*

People who have been fired or laid off are very fearful that no one's going to hire them again. In this day and age, the average employee will make 10 job changes, and with downsizing and corporate layoffs happening all over the place, you're likely to find yourself in this situation once or twice. Actually, your fear and concern are probably stronger than the employer's. I've had hundreds of clients who lost their jobs, and many went on to find better positions than the job that got away. In most instances, the fact that you were fired is not going to stop you from being hired again. But if you believe it's going to be held against you, then you can create a lot of doubt in the employer's mind just by the way you answer this question.

To prepare an answer, there are a couple of techniques that I'd suggest. First, if you were fired because of a personality conflict with another person at your former position, recognize that almost 80% of firings are the result of interpersonal conflict on the job. Incompetent workers keep their jobs, but people with personality conflicts usually, somewhere along the line, lose theirs. So if this is the reason you've been fired, then take pen and paper and write out some sample answers. Analyze what took place, why you were let go. Let's say you couldn't get along with your supervisor. You had differences of opinion, and because of those differences of opinion, the supervisor eventually made the decision to fire you. Here's how to answer this very difficult question:

"About a year ago I got a new supervisor and the company started heading in a new direction. My job duties changed and the company decided it needed different skills from what I had to offer or could learn quickly, and that's why I am available." Another approach might be: "One of the most important things that I've learned since I left my last job is the importance of having open communication. My boss was not a person that talked about goals or expectations, but instead reacted when something went wrong. I'm the type of person who likes to get feedback so that I know if I'm doing a good job, if I'm meeting expectations, or if something's going haywire, so I can work on correcting it. There was a problem with the budget process at my last job. I thought we had more time to retrieve the information than we did. The information from other areas needed to be analyzed and we had no control to speed up getting the other departments to respond faster. I created a conflict with my boss by trying to get him to go to the departments and get the information sent to us faster and in a different form. My boss felt differently and decided that because of the conflict between him and me that he should let me go. I've learned a lot since then, and I know that it's going to be very important in my new job to make sure that I find a supervisor that has open communication, is responsive, and that I work well with. If you call my former employer, he will tell you that I was a good worker, that I brought strong financial and accounting skills to the workplace, even that my supervisory ability with my other staff worked well. These strengths were never in question." As you can see, this is an answer that is well thought out. The candidate planned how to answer the question. Point out where there was a problem and where there wasn't, so the employer gets a feeling that yes, maybe you just didn't get along with that supervisor because of poor communication and weak leadership.

If you were laid off, you might respond: "My company, like so many others, has restructured, and my position was eliminated during the reorganization," or, "My company decided to close its regional office and my entire department was let go." In either answer end with: "That's why I am presently available." Be careful with this answer so that your voice and tone don't express anger or desperation. It is important that you don't appear to want just any job, but to be seeking the right opportunity. You may feel desperate, but practice *not* letting that feeling sneak into your tone. The employer wants to believe you really want *his* job, not just any job.

65. "I've noticed there was a period of time when you weren't employed. Tell me about it."

Examine your reason for the work gap. The most frequent reasons are time between employment, a personal illness, a family illness, failed self-employment, maternity leave, or raising young children. What's important here is to construct your answer to show that whatever the problem was, it has been resolved, and that your performance, attendance, and motivation will all be top-notch now. To explain children or maternity and just returning, try, "I took time off to have a child (children). I have been able to secure excellent daycare that will ensure that I'll be able to work every day and be a productive employee." Be willing to answer any follow-up questions that the employer might ask, such as: *"What will you do when the child is sick? Occasionally we need this person to work overtime—will that be a problem? What are the hours that the daycare is open? How have you prepared to handle the pressures of this position and the demands of a new family member?"* The employer's concerns center around: (1) How productive will you be? (2) Will your mind be on your work? (3) Will you be reliable? (4) What ways will your situation impact your ability to do the job—no overtime, changing hours, absenteeism, etc. Your most important goal is to learn whether or not this employer's situation will work for you. The employer expects you to show up on time and to complete your assigned workload. Employers often get leery about hiring mothers because they have often had bad experiences in the past. I hired an assistant who insisted that she'd never missed a day of work while she was pregnant or when she returned after her first child. Her reference verified this. Once hired, she immediately began to experience problems—child care for two children was very expensive; she wanted to change hours to fit her daycare schedule and reduce her costs. Unfortunately, this was at the expense of closing the office early so she could go home. She only lasted two months, and once she was let go, my boss vowed never to hire a mother again. Many employers have had a bad experience like I did. Therefore, when you are returning to work after an absence, arrange daycare that will care for mildly sick children (flus, colds) or establish a secondary system (family, friend, neighbor, spouse) that will care for the child if the care center doesn't. Be sure that you have plenty of leeway to drop off and pick up your children. That way, if you need to work a little overtime, you will be able to. Don't expect or ask employers to change the position's hours to fit your daycare schedule. If you can't work their hours, e.g., 9:00 to 6:00, then drop out of consideration for that job. It is best to be honest. Predetermine your necessary take-home salary by subtracting taxes and child-care costs. This allows you to judge potential jobs more realistically.

When answering these tricky questions, demonstrate that you have thought through the situation and found good solutions, and reassure the employer about your reliability and on-the-job productivity. Also, an employer may not ask these child-care questions, but she is thinking about them. It's best to offer a good offense by explaining the specifics of how you'll be dependable and productive at their job.

66. *"You've been unemployed for quite a while; why haven't you obtained a job before this?"*

Most job hunters underestimate the length of time the job search process requires, so they take extended vacations or regroup because they are too drained by the layoff or firing. It's important to note that the average job search can take up to six months. If you've been unemployed for more than one year, you need a very good reason. An appropriate response might be: "I did take some time to evaluate my career and focus the direction of my search. I've been actively job hunting for several months and am meeting with employers to find a position that will utilize my skills and allow me to be a contributing part of the company's team."

If the unemployment was due to a personal problem or illness, you could explain with: "A personal crisis arose in my family that required my time and energy. It was difficult emotionally and so I left my position because my focus could not be on my job. Now the situation is completely resolved. I am ready and eager to work. I feel that my previous strengths of . . . (mention two or three of your most marketable abilities) will assist me in again being an asset to my employer." Sometimes you can mention the incident—illness, divorce, death, accident—but use your judgment. No employer will believe you've completely recovered from the death of your spouse in four weeks. I believe it is best not to give many details; instead, try to move on quickly and avoid a lengthy discussion of this difficult personal issue.

Illegal Questions

Job hunters often wonder, how do you answer those illegal questions? Illegal or not, these questions still get asked. It is against the law to discriminate against an individual because of age, religion, race, nationality, gender, or skin color. But that still doesn't stop employers from asking illegal questions. I believe employers, not really skilled or trained in the art of interviewing, don't recognize that these *are* illegal questions. Some are ignorant; some just have gotten away with it in the past. But handling these questions in an interview is often quite challenging. Think about this important consideration before you answer—*Do you want this job?* The response you make is really based on whether or not you want the position. You may make a principled stand, and say, "That's an illegal question and I choose not to answer it," but you will probably offend the interviewer. That response might make the employer feel ignorant and embarrassed if he indeed didn't know that it was an illegal question. He may disqualify you as a candidate. Job hunters often claim that they feel that the employer is testing them. I find it unlikely, when lawsuits are so prevalent, that an employer would intentionally break the law. Employers who attend my seminars on the hiring interview state that they don't want to ask any illegal questions. Yet they admit that they are frustrated because there is some personal stuff that they really want to know about. My advice to you is if you are asked something illegal and you really want the job, simply answer it. Let me give you a couple of examples on handling these tricky situations.

67. *"Are you pregnant, or do you have any plans to have children in the near future?"*

This was a question I was asked when I was interviewing for a vocational counselor position at one of the state's community colleges. It was a panel interview, and I'll admit that when the gentleman asked me this question I was astounded. State job, asking an illegal question like this? I wanted this job, so I said, "At this point in time, my husband and I have no children." It was not necessary for me to elaborate on the question, but I chose to answer it that way because I was interested in the job. Later on, I was told by several people that the gentleman was from the "old school," and he just didn't realize that was an illegal question. His naïveté could have gotten the state in a lot of trouble. I had grounds to sue for gender discrimination. I was not inclined to do so. Incidentally, I did get the job.

68. *"What does your husband think about your traveling so much?"*

Just answer the question with: "Travel has always been a requirement in the previous positions that I've held. I expect it to be a part of this job." If you are not married, say: "I am not married and free to travel as needed."

69. *"What does your wife think about having to move all the way to Nebraska?"*

Careful, this employer really wants to see if you will truly move to Nebraska and what obstacles your family might impose. A recent survey in *USA Today* revealed that many employees are reluctant to relocate. Seventy-five percent cited the impact on their children as the top reason not to move. Additional concerns included disinterest in the new location, concern over spouse/partner's job, and quality-of-life issues. Relocation costs are very expensive for a company to undertake. Thus, it is imperative that you dispel the aforementioned concerns with your answer. A good reply would be: "Relocating to advance my career is a part of our family goals. Both my wife and I like the Midwest and welcome the chance to move there."

70. *"Who's going to care for your kids while you're at work?"*

Employers worry about hiring working parents. Quite often it is because some other employee caused the employer numerous problems due to family demands. Most employers want reassurance that you will be dependable and productive and will pitch in when needed. Be sure to have solid daycare arrangements in place so you can squelch any concerns. I've rarely found a case where an employer isn't understanding when something tragic happens to one of your family members, once you've been with the company for a while. But when he's hiring you, he just wants to be sure that you're going to show up. So reassure him that you are a loyal and dedicated employee, and remove any obstacles that he may have by answering with: "I have a dependable person who cares for my children even if they are ill.

She takes them to appointments and activities, and is flexible so I can work overtime when I am needed."

71. *"What country are you from?"*
You'll need to answer this question by reassuring the employer that she can legally employ you. Your answer might sound like this: "China. I have been here for several years and do have valid working papers to be employed in this country. My experience includes . . ." Then reiterate your 60 Second Sell.

72. *"The job requires you to work on Sunday. Will your religion cause a problem with that?"*
"Not at all." Nothing further need be said.

73. *"How will you adapt to this new job?"*
Just because the employer doesn't verbalize a discriminatory question doesn't mean he isn't thinking it. Here's an example that shows how a job hunter addressed the unspoken concern about his age and dispelled any preconceived ideas the employer might have held about older workers being inflexible or slow to pick up a new skill.

The candidate offered some reasonable proof that his age was an asset: "At my last job, I always proved to be very flexible and adaptable, frequently taking on new tasks and picking up new skills. I enjoy learning and teaching others. I found that when I deal with difficult customers or solve complex problems I can draw upon my extensive experience, and this has repeatedly proved to be an asset in my former positions." You could then go on to describe a specific situation where your experience led you to make the right choice where a less experienced person might have made a mistake. Conclude that with age comes experience, and often the wisdom to make better decisions.

If you are lucky, you may never be asked to answer an illegal question. If you get one, I suggest you answer the question quickly, and let the interview proceed.

Technical Expertise and Specialty Questions

It is reasonable to assume that you will be asked very specific questions related to your field. Once you've gained experience in an industry and job area, you'll need to be able to give examples and answer related questions. A computer programmer should expect numerous questions concerning the languages she knows, and the types of software and applications she has worked on. Likewise, a teacher might be asked questions about his subject, teaching style, curriculum development, and learning patterns. An event planner would likely get logistic and planning questions, and so on.

To prepare, create five to 10 questions you think you might get asked concerning your field. Then practice answering them. Again, remember the guidelines—short, concise answers of less than 60 seconds, using real work examples to demonstrate how you've done this work before.

15 Questions for College Students and New Grads

Most students have little or no related work experience when they go to the interview for their first professional job. You wonder what you should say, how you should answer those questions. Often you are very nervous. Others are workers who have returned to college for an advanced degree or to obtain their bachelor's. Many employers are out there looking for new talent, but the competition is keen, so good, thoughtful answers are essential.

Preparation can help relieve some of that anxiety and allow you to effectively communicate the skills you do have. Most often, new graduates have had only service jobs— working in a fast-food restaurant or retail store. There you've learned customer service skills and how to work under pressure. Dependability became a personal habit. Be sure to examine all your work experience and activities for evidence of leadership or business skills, organizational abilities, time management skills, and research, analysis, teamwork, or report-writing abilities. Develop your 5 Point Agenda and 60 Second Sell after you have researched and learned the job duties and skills necessary to do the employer's job. Be sure to target positions at the right level— usually entry level.

Practice answering questions with full and complete responses that get your point across in 60 seconds or less. Here are some frequently asked questions you should be able to answer effectively.

74. *"What are your long-range and short-range goals and objectives? How are you preparing yourself to achieve them?"*

The interviewer wants to see how focused you are and how realistic. The interviewer wonders about the training time that you'll need to become productive and how long you'll stay once the company has invested time training you. A good response might be an honest one. "My short-term goal is to get a job that will provide me with the training and environment to use the skills I've developed in college. I'm a very hard worker and a quick learner, so I want an environment where I can contribute. I believe that once I'm working, I'll be exposed to many areas of business that I haven't seen yet, so I plan to keep my long-term options open while I explore numerous possibilities." This response doesn't jeopardize your chances for a position by mapping out a career agenda, such as "Next year I'm off to law school," that doesn't fit into the employer's agenda. Show flexibility, adaptability, and definitely a wise attitude about your future opportunities.

75. "Describe your ideal job and location."

Tricky question, as you often don't know what your *ideal* job is and often say you'll move anywhere. Most students will move to get a job. Analyze where you will and won't move. Then respond with, "I really am willing to move wherever the company needs me, though I'm concentrating my search on the East Coast. My ideal job is in an environment that allows me to learn, gain new skills, and be a productive worker. It is also very important for me to know that I'm helping people through my efforts." Or end with, "It's important that I make a contribution to the company." You may add something that shows you're a little knowledgeable about the job. "Last summer I took an unpaid internship at the Lung Foundation. I worked on two fundraising projects and their direct mail campaign. This position gave me some insight into a career in fundraising—a job I feel is important and meaningful, and one I want to do and do well."

76. "What two or three accomplishments have given you the most satisfaction? Why?"

Here is a great opportunity to stress two or three points in your 5 Point Agenda. Let's say organizational skills are one point and time management is another. You could respond, "Graduating from college was a big accomplishment for me, and so was getting that A in statistics. I held a part-time job while attending school. I often needed to prioritize and plan out my schedule, setting aside the time to study and do papers. Statistics was a challenging course for me and required a lot of extra effort. I organized a study group and I worked on problems every day. I felt pressured by the job, but needed to work to cover tuition costs, so I cut out extra socializing for a few weeks and pulled an A. I felt like my hard work paid off in both cases, and that's been very satisfying."

77. *"What led you to choose your field or major?"*

"Liberal arts has taught me to think out problems, research and analyze data, and develop good written communication skills. I've found sociology to be interesting with its broad-based analysis of society's behavior patterns. My classes required reading eight to nine books per course, so I feel I've also developed excellent time management skills when tackling a heavy workload." Another approach is to show how your major reflects your natural abilities and passion. If you were an accounting major, your answer might be very specific, such as, "I started out in the business track and took Fundamentals of Accounting my freshman year. I loved it. I loved the analytical challenge, and I've always had a strong ability when working with numbers. I decided to be an accountant after that class and am a student member of the state CPA society. It's a field I know I will succeed in, as I've done very well in my college program."

78. *"What college subjects did you like best? Least? Why?"*

This tells the interviewer your strengths and your weaknesses, and therein lies the tricky part. Your answer must illustrate interest in areas necessary to do the company's job, and denote only subjects that are unrelated that you disliked. You could create an answer like this, substituting your favorite subject: "Psychology classes were my favorites and my major. I loved learning about human behavior, interaction, and helping others deal with behavior difficulties. I least liked the modern art class. I found it too abstract for me. I enjoyed the Renaissance period much better."

79. "Do you have plans for continued study? An advanced degree?"

Tricky question here. The interviewer is trying another avenue to access your goals and how it will fit into his organization's needs. If you do not plan to go on, simply say, "At this time, I plan to land a position and work hard to be productive. I don't have any current plans to go on." If you are planning to go on, you could say, "I plan to get two or three years of engineering work first, and then I think I'd like to enroll in an evening MBA program. I know that it's very demanding to handle both, but I think I can, as I worked all through college. I do feel it is important now to move from the classroom to a manufacturing setting because there's a lot to learn on the job before I pursue more education."

80. "In what part-time or summer jobs have you been most interested? Why?" (Situational)

Most part-time jobs are not interesting and you often worked just for the money. Try to answer the question by noting something you did like, for example, "I lived in a small town and was very lucky to get any job. I worked as a receptionist for a real estate office. I enjoyed talking to people who called, especially when I could answer their questions or solve their problem. The best part of my job was a small two-week project I worked on. Their secretary got sick and I did a large spreadsheet project for them. My boss was thrilled I could enter data and that I knew Excel. I spent extra hours on my own time learning some advances in the program so I could make the tables easy for everyone to use. I really enjoyed that and want a position that requires a lot of computer work."

81. **"What have you learned from the jobs you've had?"**

The answer is your 60 Second Sell as it relates to jobs and not course work. Or you could say, "I've learned how important it is to be on time, to be at work every day, and to work hard while I'm there. When I was a waitress, it really made it hard on everyone if another waitress called in sick. One night I had all the tables because both other waitresses didn't show up. It was a very high pressure, intense night. I worked hard and fast, but was tremendously overloaded. Anyone else would have quit. But I knew that the employer was counting on me, so I worked that night alone. I also learned that it's crucial to make every effort to be at the job *every* day."

82. **"If you were on an eight-hour transatlantic flight, who would you want to sit next to you and what would you talk about?"**

The interviewer is interested in having you reveal more of your personality, your depth, and your personal interests. Resist saying the current movie star hearthrob or model because he or she is so gorgeous. Better to illustrate depth and to think before you answer. Select someone that could teach you something. A notable businessperson or political figure is a good choice. A business student could say, "Bill Gates. I'm fascinated by Microsoft's products and the company as a whole. I think he's a true visionary. I would spend the time learning about the roles he thinks computers will play in the future, the information technology changes he foresees, and how that will impact our whole society and the way we conduct business."

83. **"How do you think a former boss or professor who knows you well would describe you?"**

Sell yourself through your boss or professor's eyes by saying, "They would tell you . . . ," and then go into your 60

Second Sell. Adding that you're a conscientious, hard worker is always a plus too.

84. *Riddles*
Several high-tech companies pride themselves on asking for the solutions to very difficult riddles. Some of these riddles have no correct answers at all. The interviewer is interested in your thought pattern and processing skills. Listen carefully and ask the interviewer to repeat the riddle. Be thoughtful and reply. If you don't know, admit it and say, "I'd need to check (a reference guide) to find the correct answer."

85. *"If you were an animal, what would you be?"*
There is no right answer—a tiger, a lion, a bear, a dolphin—so just try to relate the animal to the skills needed to do the job. For example, aggressive sales equals quick, responsive, and fast, so you might say a tiger, offering those traits as the reason. Your job does not depend on offering the right animal, so don't sweat this one.

86. *"If you are a part of a salad, what part are you?"*
Again, another wasted question that doesn't provide evidence of job skills. But then, no one said the interviewer will only ask smart questions. A good response might be: "I'd be the lettuce—it's the basic essential part without which you wouldn't have a salad."

87. *"Give me an example of when you've demonstrated your customer service skills on the job."*
   (Situational)
"At McDonald's I worked the drive-through window. You need to be polite, accurate, fast, and efficient or the customers can really pile up. I always double-checked the order on the screen by repeating it out loud to reaffirm it's what

the customer wanted and eliminate mistakes that would make customers angry."

88. *"Give me an example of a time you've worked on a team or in a group." (Situational)*

"As a communications major, I needed to take Advertising 101. Our class grade was based on a group project. We were put into five groups, six per group. I was the team leader, and we divided up the workload. One person fell behind and didn't do the work. Everyone got angry at this person and told me to "force him" to do it. Instead, I went to my professor and asked for ideas on ways I could motivate my teammate. I thought about my teacher's suggestions and talked it over with the person. He didn't understand how to find the research, so I and a few others helped him clarify the steps, and soon his work was on a par with everyone else's. We all ended up with an A, and I'm proud of how we did work together to complete the project and make the grade."

89. *"Give me an example of a problem you've had here at college and how you solved it." (Situational)*

"I changed my major at the start of my sophomore year to business and needed an economics course. The class that fit into my schedule was full, so I went to the first three sessions, talked to the professor, and convinced him to let me in so I wouldn't get behind in my prerequisites. Incidentally, I got an A– in that class."

Do Your Best

Preparing for potential questions in advance will give you a big advantage over the numerous job hunters who do not prepare. When you write out answers, you have time to analyze the difficult questions and calmly select effective answers that demonstrate to the employer that you can and will do her job well. Actually, the reason people think questions are tough or difficult is that they haven't really thought about them. They got stumped because they had no plan to follow, no previous ideas jotted down. Short, concise answers of less than 60 seconds that avoid the minefields can result in *you* landing the job. Your interview is really where the employer decides whether or not to hire you. Work hard to do your best. You will not win every time, but you'll improve with each interview and get better at effectively marketing your abilities. Always remember our mantra—60 Seconds and You're Hired!

There are two things to aim at in life:

first to get what you want

and after that to enjoy it.

Only the wisest of men achieve both.

Chapter 6

Questions You Should Ask

At some point in every interview the employer will ask, "Do you have any questions?" This is your opportunity to determine that this job, company, and boss are a good place for you. Often the candidate searches to ask just anything, appearing dumb to the interviewer because he did not prepare his own list of questions in advance. This will not happen to you. Take the time before the interview to think about what information you need to aid you in deciding if this is a good fit for you. This is a very important part of the interviewing process. The employer often puts a lot of weight on what you ask. People have a hard time thinking up their questions. The questions *you* want to ask are strictly job-related and duty-related. You can ask all about the company's benefits, sick leave, pension programs, *after* you've gotten the job offer.

How to Impress the Employer

Hiring managers repeatedly tell me that they pay particular attention to the questions that applicants ask them. Your questions, especially when they are insightful, send a signal that you are not only interested in the job but truly trying to evaluate whether this will be a good match and work out long-term for both parties. A top manager at AT&T said: "I judge candidates by the questions they ask. That's what's most revealing to me. I want someone focused on succeeding in the job and not just centered on how much money I will pay him."

Before the interview, prepare a list of pertinent questions that you would like answered to determine if this position is really a good job for you. Write or type out your questions on a piece of paper that you can take out when it's your turn to ask questions. The employer is impressed that you cared enough about his position to think through his organization's needs and duties. Do not bring up any questions about salary or benefits at this time. Focus on determining if you want to do this job. Your questions also give insight into your thoroughness when given important responsibilities. Create your list of questions beforehand. Ten to 15 questions are a reasonable number to have on your list. Many will have been answered during the interview. Bring up anything the employer mentioned that you want to know more about. If by chance he has already answered every question, say this: "As I check over my list, my questions on your software were covered as well as the equipment you use. We discussed budgets and training policies. I guess you've covered everything already."

Gaining Insight on Their Corporate Culture

Every organization has a workplace environment that defines what it is actually like to work there. Prior to the interview, you may have preconceived ideas about the company's culture based on its marketing and advertising, or on media news.

Often these preconceived ideas prove to be inaccurate once you get into the interview and begin to ask your questions. Better to learn now that you don't want this job, rather than three weeks after you've started. Therefore, pay close attention to the answers and whether this is a boss you would like to work with daily.

You can't always have prepared all your questions in advance since they often arise as a result of a part of the interview. It's often best to ask these questions as soon as they come up, saying, "Could you explain that more fully," or "Please elaborate." Be sure you get answers to incongruities and to learn more if a red flag comes up. Use your detective skills to determine what the true workplace environment will be and if it's a comfortable fit for you.

37 Questions You Could Ask

Here are 37 questions that you can consider asking. Notice how each one is designed to gather details on doing the job and learning more about the organization's work culture and environment. Be sure to pose the appropriate question to the correct person. Technical questions and job specifics are unlikely to be answered by the HR person, whose responsibility is to screen and validate your true experience, but who possesses only a general idea of the job duties. By the end of your questions with the hiring manager or decision maker you should know whether or not you want to work there.

- *"What are the day-to-day responsibilities that I'll have in this job?"*
- *"Whom will I be supervising?"*
- *"Could you explain your organizational structure to me?"*

- *"What is the organization's plan for the next five years, and how does this department or division fit in?"*
- *"Will we be expanding, bringing on any new products or new services that I should be aware of?"*
- *"Could you describe to me your typical management style and the type of employee that works well with you?"*
- *"What are some of the skills and abilities you see as necessary for someone to succeed in this job?"*
- *"What challenges might I encounter if I take on this position?"*
- *"What are your major concerns that need to be immediately addressed in this job?"*
- *"What are the areas in the job that you'd like to see improved?"*
- *"What is your company's policy on providing seminars, workshops, and training so the employees can keep up on their skills or acquire new skills?"*
- *"What is the budget this department operates with?"*
- *"Are there any restraints or cutbacks planned that would decrease those budgets?"*
- *"What particular computer equipment and software do you use here? When was your last upgrade?"*
- *"Are any new equipment purchases planned?"*
- *"What personality traits do you think are necessary to succeed in this job?"*
- *"Will I be working as part of a team or alone?"*
- *"What committees will I participate in?"*
- *"How will my leadership responsibilities and performance be measured? By whom?"*
- *"To what extent are the functions of this department considered important by upper management?"*
- *"Are there any weaknesses in the department that you are working to improve?"*

- *"What are the company's long-term goals?"*
- *"What are the department's goals and how do they fit into the company's mission?"*
- *"What are the company's strengths and weaknesses compared to its competition?"*
- *"How does the reporting structure work here? What are acceptable channels of communication?"*
- *"What new endeavors is the company currently undertaking?"*
- *"What goals or objectives need to be achieved in the next six months? Next year?"*
- *"What areas of the job would you like to see improvement in with regard to the person who was most recently performing these duties?"*
- *"Would I encounter any coworker or staff person who's proved to be a problem in the past? If yes, please explain."*
- *"Describe the atmosphere of the office." (You are looking for clues on pressure and stress level with this question.)*
- *"What types of people seem to excel here?"*
- *"Is the company quick or slow to adapt to new technology?"*
- *"How would you describe the politics of this organization?"*
- *"Can you give me an idea of the typical workload and extra hours or special needs it demands?"*
- *"Where is the person who previously held this job?" (If fired, ask why; if promoted, where did he or she go; if at a new job, get a better idea of why it was created.)*
- *"How does the company promote personal and professional growth?"*
- *"How would you describe the corporate culture here?"*

Ideally, you need to stay focused on the job—the duties and/or the promotional opportunities. A key strategy is to not ask questions about the salary, benefits, or perks. The best time to cover those issues is *after* you've been offered the job.

The difference between great and average is how often you take risks. Calculated risks that temporarily force you to live outside your comfort zone often result in Big Wins.

Chapter 7

Salary Questions

The hardest questions can be those that deal with salary. Handling them like a pro can assure you of obtaining the highest offer possible from an employer.

Salary History

Want ads request salary history about one quarter of the time. Applications commonly ask for previous salary information. Why? To screen applicants OUT. This screening tool has nothing to do with your exceptional abilities to do the job—only the dollars-and-cents cost. The best strategy to deal with this is simply to send nothing. Leave any salary requests blank. Employers have been known to increase the salary, change the job title, or add more benefits, paying thousands more than they initially set forth, in order to hire the person that they *want* for the job. Job hunters eliminate themselves from consideration not only when their salary history is high, but also if it appears to be too low. The employer concludes that the candidate is not as good as the resumé says or he would be making more money. A trick some employers use to get you to reveal your salary history is to state in the ad: *Send salary history, those without it won't be considered.* This can be responded to in your cover letter by adding a line or two at the end that cites a professional group or magazine's salary survey that offers a range. For example, "The most recent Women in Communication survey states that a public relations specialist like myself with ten years of experience for an agency makes between $45,000 and $70,000, and that's the range I'm in."

Secrets of Establishing Your Value

Always, always, always—establish your value first. People want what they want. Employers too. That's the psychology that becomes your competitive edge in the salary negotiations process when you are the one they want. Once the employer decides he must have *you* to do the work, there is a role reversal. Now he needs to recruit and sell you on taking the job. It all begins with knowing what your skills and abilities are worth, then communicating that value to an employer. The end result is that the employer *must* have you to do the job.

How to Learn What They Will Pay

To accurately assess your value in the workplace, I suggest that you conduct an investigation into what comparable jobs pay for the job title you are looking for in your geographical area. There are several places to find this information. Associations and business magazines frequently publish annual salary surveys. They often break down salary by job title, level of experience, and geographical region. The Department of Labor publishes numerous salary lists. Many such surveys are posted on career websites. Your best bet is to ask the reference librarian to help you find the salary information you seek. Websites continuously change, and reference librarians stay on top of the best ways to find the latest salary surveys. These reference folks are a great time saver. Lastly, consider asking colleagues this question: *"I'm seeking a new position as an electrical engineer for a manufacturing company. I have five years' experience. I expect a salary of $55,000. Do you think that is reasonable? Would it be reasonable for your company?"* Another technique is to ask, *"What is the typical range this job would pay in your company?"* Gather the facts early so you can have a reasonable expectation of the salary you could obtain. Be sure to include like-size employers—nonprofits and small employers will often pay less than their larger counterparts.

Answering the Question

90. *"What salary do you expect if we offer you the job?"*

Too often, job hunters just throw out a number. That is a critical mistake. Always remember that the first person who mentions money loses. Loses in terms of real dollars. And in your case, sometimes loses the job. If we use the psychology of people wanting what they want, we must first make them want us. So try these answers: "I expect to be fairly compensated for my work. I feel confident that if we determine I'm the right person to do the job, we can reach an agreement. To me, it's the job itself that is most important." This approach can often encourage an employer to move on.

A more persistent interviewer may say, *"Well, we need to determine salary expectations. What figure do you expect?"* Here's where my Salary Extractor technique works well. Answer with, "What is the salary range that this position pays?" This volleyball technique encourages her to give you the figure. Typically she will say, "It pays $35,000 to $40,000." You respond, "I'm within your range," or if it is low, "I'm near that range," and then go on with the interview. Try to avoid lengthy salary discussions. At this stage in the interview, mention a figure that's too low and the employer will think you certainly must lack the skills to do her job. If you are too high then she'll believe you'd never work for less. The interviewer will quickly determine you are not the one she wants based on these answers alone.

Your winning strategy is this—keep the conversation centered on how well you can do the job. Continually promote your 5 Point Agenda. Utilize your 60 Second Sell whenever appropriate. These will market your best strengths and influence the employer to decide she *must* have you. Once the job offer has been formally made, THEN it's the right time to discuss and negotiate the salary you want and deserve for performing that job.

Success can be yours,
but nothing happens by itself.
It will all come your way
once you understand
that you have to make it
come your way
by your own efforts.
When opportunity knocks,
be ready.

Chapter 8

Negotiating the Best Deal

As the employer says, "You got the job," you mumble some pleasantry as you silently scream, "YES!" If you intend to negotiate for any benefits or salary increase, then as tempting as it is to just accept, I advise you to refrain from that outburst and say, "I'd like to meet with you tomorrow to discuss your offer and all the details." If he hasn't stated the salary, ask it. Arrange the meeting time. If you are on the phone, end the conversation. If you are face-to-face, try to reset for the next day if possible. You have a lot of preparation to do, especially if you want the employer to raise the offer. This meeting you just arranged is called the Negotiations Interview, and there is a formula to follow to successfully negotiate a better compensation package.

Men and Women Negotiate Differently

Women still make 23% less than men, according to the Department of Labor. Much of this is due to the fact that men often try to negotiate salary whereas women typically accept the original offer as given. Client after client after client has proven that she can improve the original offer by following the negotiation strategies that follow. Women must change their thinking from the sociologically ingrained "Be polite, be humble, be grateful, be a pleaser" and move beyond her comfort zone and act like a competitive candidate who expects top dollar and benefits in exchange for her talents.

Biggest Raises Come with a New Job

Many people use the opportunity to secure a new job as the chance to move up into a promotional position and secure more money. *The biggest salary increases almost always are the result of changing jobs and companies.* These can range from 10 to 30%. Some of my clients have seen 40 to 50% increases. And a few clients have actually doubled their salaries. When you pursue the opportunity to move on to a new organization, you should expect it to be a profitable, and in some instances a *very* profitable, move.

More Employers Negotiating the Whole Compensation Package

During the last 18 months employers have shown more latitude in negotiating salaries than ever before during the 20 years I've been a career counselor. It seems almost as if just by asking, people get thousands of dollars more plus extra perks, such as more vacation. One CEO summed it up this way: "We have to have talent to move ahead. People are more aware of their value these days and it's a struggle to find good people. We must offer a competitive salary— what's a few thousand more if they are the perfect match for the job?"

Moral of the story: ASK.

Determine the Risks

Salary negotiations are a game—a sophisticated game, but a game nonetheless. You must enter this playing arena fully equipped with facts, influential information, and effective negotiation strategies to follow.

Your first step is to assess the employer's compensation style.

Fixed Offer. Some employers simply do not negotiate. They offer a take-it-or-leave-it deal. They have a set limit on how much that job is worth to them.

Pay Grade System. A predetermined range is set for the job, based on duties required. Where you fall in this range is determined by your years of experience. This system rarely offers the top salary to anyone; it is earned in raises over the years. To significantly raise the salary, the employer often has to reclassify the job in a higher pay grade. This has been known to happen, especially when it has been established that the employer underestimated the skills necessary to adequately perform the job.

Negotiable Guidelines. This is the best situation. The employer has more liberty to raise or lower the salary as he sees fit. This allows you the best chance to bargain for your services.

Your next step is to assess the job market's supply of qualified candidates. If there are others who are equally qualified and the employer would be happy with any of them, this is a clue that your negotiating power is reduced. Then again, I've seen clients sail right to the top of a stack of 400 resumés and then land the job. The employer really wanted them and so they were able to secure excellent compensation packages in spite of the competition. They argued that they were the best of the lot. The employer agreed, and paid dearly to have them join his team.

The final step before you begin the face-to-face negotiations is to determine what is a fair offer, particularly if you've been overpaid or underpaid. During your salary survey, you should have determined what is a fair compensation. When leaving a large Fortune 500 company for a smaller organization, you can expect a smaller offer. Yet sometimes, after having spent years merely getting cost-of-living raises, you are making less than the going market rate. When moving from an underpaid situation, how much more is enough? Small employers often offer less salary and fewer benefits in exchange for more responsibility and interesting, challenging jobs. Cautiously determine the employer's compensation style. *Asking* for more compensation properly rarely risks an offer being withdrawn, but *demanding* more can. Predetermine a *fair, reasonable* goal for both you and the employer, and then use the negotiation strategies to get what you want (maybe even much more than you'd hoped for).

Negotiation Strategies

When you arrive at the negotiation interview, implement these techniques in your efforts to get the best deal.

1. *Confident Approach*

Your tone often affects the results of this whole process. Exude enthusiasm for the job. Reconfirm your ability to do the job. Have a win/win attitude. To begin the conversation, ask about the benefits, vacations, and overtime. Grill the employer on all these terms. Ask what is policy and what is practiced. Often the policy is that you receive compensation time for your overtime hours. The practice may be that you are absolutely discouraged from ever using it. Learn the rules and practices.

To lead into the discussion about salary, say, "I'm really

interested in the position. I was a little disappointed because the offer was lower than I expected." Then be quiet and remain quiet while the employer makes the next move. Another approach is, "I'm very interested in the job; is there a possibility of negotiating here?" Smile and follow the employer's lead.

2. Negotiate to Get the Money Up Front

Bonuses, raises, and reviews in a few months all have a way of never happening down the line. Every dollar you negotiate into the base salary now is more money you can spend on things you and your family want. Work toward the extra money up front. These negotiations could give you in minutes what would take years to achieve with raises.

3. Try

Most people are afraid to try, especially women and unemployed people. Women tend to devalue themselves. They don't recognize their complete worth in the workplace and rarely demand it. Salary studies reveal that women are still paid substantially lower than men because women allow it. I encourage every person to expect and seek comparable compensation for the job performed.

The unemployed person sits in a difficult spot. He or she often needs the job, and the employer knows it. In this situation, reiterate what you bring and try to get a fair compensation. Often the employer will give a lowball offer just to see if you will take it. Test the waters to see if there is room for the employer to pay more. It doesn't hurt to mention that there are other companies interested in your talents if you've been actively interviewing.

4. Settle for the Middle

Negotiations often end with both sides compromising. Allow room to do just that. If the employer offers $52,000 and you want $55,000, try this: "We're pretty close in terms of salary. I was thinking with my 10 years of experience that $57,000 is more in line." Be willing to give a little—if you get $55,000 you'll still be $3,000 ahead of the $52,000 originally offered. Sometimes employers take your lead and agree to the figure you have suggested.

5. *Money and What Else?*

Compensation benefits come in very complex packages ranging from nothing at all to free daycare services. Evaluate the extra value a company's retirement plan adds. What about vacation time, flexible hours, tuition reimbursement, fewer hours, days off, relocation expenses, stock options, company car, expense accounts, bonuses? Perhaps the salary cannot be raised, but additional benefits can be added. Look closely at the medical plan. What kind of coverage is provided? What deductibles does the plan include? Who pays for dependents? If you pay, what will that cost be? My clients have successfully argued for a higher salary to compensate for switching medical plans where the old employer covered the entire family and the new one covers just the employee. Predetermine which benefits are important to you and negotiate for them.

Vacations and days off can often be negotiated. Be careful because other staff often resent favoritism to a new employee. And just because you had four weeks' vacation from your last position (with 10 years of service), it is unlikely the new company will give you four weeks. Be flexible, be reasonable, and inquire if there's anything more the company can do. Numerous employers respond by offering an additional week or two.

6. *Focus on the Employer's Needs*

Resell yourself throughout this process. Reaffirm the reasons they want you, the skills you'll bring, and how you will solve their problems. Mention your 60 Second Sell and stress how quickly you will be productive. In other words, give them reasons to pay you more. This is an important strategy, since the interviewer may need to go to her boss and to personnel to obtain the approval to pay you more. By offering her ammunition—for example, "My experience with your systems is an asset"—she can likewise tell her boss and come back with a higher offer.

One very effective technique that I've had clients use is to create a chart (I call it the Hiring Chart) that outlines the job "needs" and your abilities to do the job, your "contributions." On the next page is an actual Hiring Chart a client used in her salary negotiations.

Use your Hiring Chart to go over with the employer *her* needs and detail your past accomplishments and potential contribution. Let the employer keep this chart. It's proof of why she should pay you more, and it's a great tool for her to go to upper management and explain why you are worth the extra dollars.

7. *Know Your Bottomline*

Only you can decide when the offer is too low. There will be other offers, but they may be weeks down the road. Never bluff the potential employer though. Offers can be withdrawn when a job hunter says, "Thirty-six thousand dollars is as low as I will accept." Be prepared to keep looking. Sometimes that is the right move for you. Decide what is the lowest you can reasonably accept to cover your bills and concentrate on succeeding in the job and not immediately start looking for another, higher-paying one.

8. *Practice*

Think through the negotiation interview. Visualize a successful outcome. Then ask a friend to role-play the interviewer. Defend why you are worth the money. Listen to the

Patty Smith
Director of Promotions

NEEDS	CONTRIBUTIONS
Creative	12 years in creative services.
Promotions	Promotion/advertising for #1 independent TV station in L.A. using direct mail, publicity campaign, sales presentation, and special events.
Writing	Press releases, bios, on-air promotions, business proposals.
Public Relations	Extensive experience working with print, broadcast, media, celebrities, agencies.
Budgets	Budgets/advertising for TV station in L.A. emphasizing cost-effective spending.
Events	Coordinator for Sammy Davis Jr.'s 60th birthday video, coordinated special gallery exhibitions, organized celebrity appearances.
Supervision	Trained staff. Easily coordinate others into a cohesive team.
Client/Customer Relations	Developed new business. Built solid, long-lasting client relationships.
Sponsorship	Excellent research skills to develop prospect list for joint sponsorship and events to maximize visibility.
Sales	Able to prospect, evaluate leads, write proposals, and close sales effectively.

feedback—did you convince your friend? This preparation will decrease your anxiety and increase your confidence.

9. *Employment Letter*

Once you have agreed upon all the terms, ask for an employment letter. You can offer to write it or the employer can, but be sure the employer signs it. This letter should outline all the terms of your employment. Cover salary, signing bonuses, stock options, starting date, and benefits; particularly note anything different from the organization's normal policies. Too many promises are made and quickly forgotten once you start the job. Get the details in writing so there are no misunderstandings later.

10. *Multiple Offers*

Oh, the luxury of choices. Be *sure* there is another choice. Once a firm offer is made, job hunters become convinced that the other organization they just interviewed for wants them also. Does it? Employers don't like to be pushed because you have "other offers." A straightforward approach works best. Call the other employers with whom you interviewed and tell them you have a firm offer. Ask them for a status report. Tell them your timeline and wait. If they are going to make you a firm offer, they will within that time limit. Sometimes you are not their first choice and they will say so. Either way, you will know where you stand. A job in hand is a real job—not a hope, dream, or belief. Decide with facts, not wishful thinking.

When two solid offers stand, decide which one you want and then negotiate hard for the best terms the company you want to work for can offer, making them aware that they are bidding against another company for your services.

How It Works

There are a number of ways to get your needs met in the salary negotiation process. Here are some examples from people I have counseled and taught:

When Jessica told the potential employer, "Considering my 12 years of expertise in association management, I thought your offer was a little on the low side." She admitted to me that remaining quiet was the hardest thing she'd ever done. The employer responded: "Oh, I know we can do better—personnel makes us offer a low-end figure just to see if you'll take it. Many do, you know." The next morning, when this employer called back, Jessica was $6,000 richer.

Sometimes the salary's acceptable but the benefits, particularly the vacation, are not. This happened in Bob's case, and he phrased his concern this way: "Your salary is in the range of what I expected. But after having 25 vacation days these last several years, it was a long reach to go back to 10. It seems to me 10 days is great for a beginner in the field, but for someone with all my experience and the accomplishments I bring to the table, it seems too much of a slip backward. With the career progression should also come more vacation, to my way of thinking." The employer responded: "What do you think is fair?" And Bob replied, "Eighteen to 20 days is fair in my mind."

The employer had a reputation for being rigid and yet he surprised us both when he came back with 18 vacation days. Bob took the job and has been a great asset to the company ever since.

Many people are able to get a signing bonus simply by saying, "What about a signing bonus?" When Michael was reluctant to accept a promising job offer, he shared his reasons for hesitating with the hiring manager: "If I stay at my current job, I've got a major $30,000 bonus due on January 1. I'm tempted to take your job, but this is a significant stumbling block—could I maybe get some kind of signing bonus?" The result was a $20,000 signing bonus and $10,000 more in stock options. He took the job and is glad he did; he now has a challenging, fun position, and the stock options have made him a very rich man.

Sandra graduated from a good school and began looking for a social work job that would pay well. She interviewed with a small agency and was thrilled when they offered her the job—until she learned how low the salary was. She consulted with me after her best efforts were met with the response, "This is all we can pay for the job." Sandra really liked the position and the boss, who had a good reputation as an excellent social worker. I pointed out to Sandra that in her first job after college, working under a boss who would teach her a lot would be a valuable asset in launching her career. She took the job, and under the boss's tutelage has become a good social worker herself. Incidentally, she just moved on to a great new job, ahead of her friends, and did negotiate a better offer this time around. Sometimes it's important to know what's the best thing for your career (and your long-term happiness) and to use that as a decision-making guideline.

Your four keys to salary negotiation success include:

- Asking for a fair price
- Continuously selling yourself and reiterating your worth
- Remembering that whoever mentions money first loses
- Evaluating your long-term goals and the career growth or security this opportunity offers

Some people may succeed because

they are destined to,

but most people succeed

because they are determined to.

Chapter 9

14 Types of Interviews

When the employer calls to say, "We'd like you to come in for an interview," it's important to respond with three questions. First, ask: "Certainly, may I ask what dates and times you have available?" You are probing to determine how many people they are talking to. Try to be the first or last person on any given day. When you are sandwiched between others, the interviews often get hurried, with less time for important notes in between. Plus the interviewer gets bored. At the end of a day, you must show enthusiasm and smile warmly, as the interviewer may be tired. Always use the 60 Second Sell to quickly develop rapport and interest and leave the employer with a lasting impression.

The next question to ask is about the type of interview. Try to gather as much information as possible. Try, "Whom will I be interviewing with?" Note the interviewer's name and title. Probe to see if the person will share more information about the job duties. Ask if a complete job description is available. If yes, have that faxed to your nearest local fax machine to aid you in your preparation. Finally, get clear directions to their office, and inquire about parking if you plan to drive.

Here are some insights to help you deal with the various types of interviews you might encounter.

Screening Interview

This initial interview is designed to narrow the pool of acceptable candidates and determine whom to call in for a full interview. This is often conducted by a human resource person or company recruiter; it is almost always on a one-to-one basis. A popular way to do this is via telephone. (One of my clients faced a conference call with three board members, so that can happen, but it's rare.)

Let's discuss a telephone interview first. The interviewer knows she will catch you off guard. She often calls in the evening or on the weekend. I've personally conducted a lot of these for employers, and I'm amazed how many people agree to talk even when there is a TV, loud children, or other distractions in the background. Preparation is the key to success, and this screening is the first hurdle along the way. When you get this call, tell the person you are just finishing something and ask if you can call back in 10 minutes. Then prepare yourself. Find a quiet spot, get your resumé out, and think about the questions the interviewer will ask. The employer's objective is to clarify experience and salary expectations. Mentally rehearse your answers. Have a pen and paper in front of you. Jot down the interviewer's name and take notes as she asks you a question. Smile, so your voice sounds friendly. Her job is to screen and validate applicants' backgrounds. She needs to hear that you have the experience to do the job. Demonstrate that you do with answers that offer examples of your past performance, and express your 5 Point Agenda. Be concise—keep your answers to less than 60 seconds. Above all, sound interested and enthusiastic about the job. The worst thing you can do is to sound monotonal, uninterested, and dull.

The screening interview seeks to weed out the unqualified and overpriced. The disadvantage is that the human resource person often is not familiar with all the details of the job. Such people are generalists and seek to validate job experience, not job potential. Be sure to structure answers to demonstrate how you have done the work in the past. Your 60 Second Sell will be effective in outlining your strengths. These interviews usually last 20 minutes. To move to the next level you must convince this person that you *can* do the job. Prepare accordingly.

In-person screening sessions require the same prep work as a telephone interview. Expect the interviewer (usually an HR person) to clarify experience, work-history details, and salary and to probe any inconsistencies or gaps. Your appearance and professional demeanor are also being noted, so present yourself in the best possible light.

Hiring Interview

This is a face-to-face, one-on-one interview. This format allows you to build rapport and establish a base to judge your potential boss, who is most often the person conducting the interview. The person may be a well-trained interviewer, typically found in large, progressive companies. Most often, the person has no formal interview training, and may ask irrelevant questions or talk too long. Always help him by offering leading information. A client interviewed with a manager who spent 20 minutes talking about the job. She took notes. She asked questions and then used the information to vary one aspect of her 60 Second Sell. Another client exclaimed that it seemed that the interviewer would never let her speak. After 30 minutes, she offered this comment, nodding her head in agreement: "I understand why customer service skills are so important to you. In my last position, I rewrote our customer service policy. My research supported the facts that our clients were dissatisfied with busy phone lines and untrained staff. I implemented a new system that answered calls more quickly. Then I developed a training program with manual and practice phone sessions. We saw a vast improvement over this last year. What do you feel needs to be done here?" If nothing else, this person took control, and showed the employer that she heard his concern, understood, and could solve his problems. It can be necessary to direct the questioning to your strengths, where you can demonstrate solutions as this client did.

All one-on-one interviews require a firm handshake, a smile, eye contact, enthusiasm, and rapport-building demeanor—open and self-confident, sending the message that you can solve the employer's problems and do the job.

Second Interview

This is usually either with the same person or with someone else in upper management, usually the first interviewer's boss.

You have gathered information at the first interview and should be clear about the employer's true needs. Often, only two or three top candidates remain for this position. Prepare and adjust your 60 Second Sell with answers to address the employer's true needs. Refer whenever possible to something the interviewer noted in the first meeting. Show enthusiasm and give examples. This employer wants to get to know you better. He wants to learn about you and your personality, and to determine if he still likes you. He wants to confirm whether you are the best fit available. Work to assure him with examples and work samples. Demonstrate an understanding for his needs and how you can offer solutions.

The boss's boss looks more globally. How do you fit into the big picture? Will you be promotion material? Are you flexible, adaptable, willing to become the worker they need today and tomorrow? Some worry that you will want a promotion too soon, and they want someone to stay and do the job they are trying to hire for. You must show your ability to meet company goals, to be productive and easy to work with. You absolutely must convince this person you can do the job and are very willing to do it. Show enthusiasm for the position and pride in your past accomplishments. Ask questions about the company's future and how the job and the division fits into the company's short- and long-term goals.

Multiple Interviews

Key positions—CEOs, vice presidents, presidents, CFOs, sales managers, human resource directors, information systems managers, marketing and advertising directors—often go through a lengthy multimeeting process. So do many middle-management jobs. You will most likely meet several key executives, and the process may take six to 10 hours. Companies feel that this extensive courtship time allows them to uncover both your strengths and your true weaknesses, and to determine whether or not they can live with those failings. A challenge in this process is that each person often has a slightly different agenda. Try to analyze each person by job title and predetermine his or her concerns. Think about how you would interact with each of them, and prepare answers and your 60 Second Sell accordingly. Many companies also have you meet with your potential staff. They put a

lot of weight on the staff comments—be open and friendly
with any staff. Clearly explain what you are like as a manager
and learn what they like. Stress that you treat everyone fairly.
Watch for any workplace disharmonies—they often are a red
flag that there is a staff conflict. Try not to discuss them in the
interview; just reiterate that you treat people fairly. You may
feel that this tension is a reason you do not want to pursue the
job. If you are still interested, you should wait to discuss and
learn about the staff conflicts until the negotiation interview,
gaining direction from top management on their expectations about how to deal with the problem.

Panel Interview

This type of interview is often challenging because it is difficult to determine who has the ultimate decision-making
power, not to mention that it is intimidating to face several
people with varying agendas and questions. Topics easily
switch from one question to the next, eliminating the flow
and rapport that is easier to create when you're speaking to
only one person.

If possible, try to determine who has the final decision-
making power and always address that person's needs and
concerns overall. Typically, this will be your potential
boss—always be certain you know which person that is.
Create your answers and your 60 Second Sell as if you were
speaking only to this person.

There will be times when you will not know who is the
true decision maker. Address your answers to the group, but
focus your answers in relation to what you think your boss
and her boss's needs will be.

When you enter the room, if possible, shake hands
firmly and smile as you are introduced to each person. Mention their names. If a table separates you, nod as you greet

each person by name, such as, "Hello, Tom," "Nice to meet you, Mary," "Bob." Address the answer to the person who asks the question. Be sure to answer the question. Qualify the question if you want more information before you answer. Look directly at the person as you respond. Good eye contact with the person asking the question is vital during this entire process.

Group Interview

This is a screening interview often used by employers when numerous applicants must actually be seen to determine a candidate's potential. You will be interviewed along with several other candidates. The airlines commonly use this type of interview when hiring flight attendants. The purpose is twofold. First, do you meet the physical requirements for the job, such as height, weight, and physical agility? Next, how outgoing, comfortable, and confident are you in a group situation? Because this process is designed to determine those with poor communication and interpersonal skills, practice speaking clearly, firmly, and with a friendly tone. Don't be surprised when you get only a couple of opportunities to answer questions. Radiate confidence that you can effectively deal with the demanding public and that you are cool, calm, and collected in high-pressure situations. These traits are imperative to doing the job well, and this intimidating format seems to aid the employer in a speedy elimination process.

Promotion Interview

"Promoting from within" is a common practice at many companies. Your knowledge of company policies, practices, and procedures is seen as a big plus. It's a fatal error to assume you will automatically be moved up, however. You must treat this critical interview as if you were going to a new organization. After all, the new job is often with a different boss or department. Craft your 5 Point Agenda and 60 Second Sell. Do research on what colleagues at similar companies are doing in the job you hope to land. Read the trade journals and search the Web for industry news. Don't let an outsider show you up—read up so you can be more global in your approach and answers. Many internal candidates lose the job by failing to do this homework. Demonstrating the ideal worker persona is critical here. Offer examples of how you took on new tasks, and are flexible and adaptable. Bring samples of your work that illustrate your skills to do the new job. If it's a move into management, discuss any volunteer or team projects you've headed up. The company wants evidence that you can firmly and effectively manage the work of others.

If you are the only internal candidate, stress that you'll bring new ideas while not taking six months to learn the company like an outsider would. You'll be productive from day one. Then comment on two or three immediate problems or concerns you'll tackle.

In some situations, a long-term employee takes on the "acting job," for example, acting director, while a search is under way. Use this time to do your best, but with no real authority from management, your results may be minimal. "Fresh blood" often seems to be management's solution, since "acting" employees typically don't bring up great ideas, solutions, or outside insights during the promotion interview. Unfortunately, many fail because they were not thorough in their preparation and did not discuss real changes they would make. Display your best so the decision maker gives you a promotion (and of course a raise too).

Stress Interview

These have become less common as employers have gotten more skilled in hiring and recognize there is a need to recruit as well as eliminate. Silence is the stress technique many interviewers commonly use. Silence makes most job hunters nervous and encourages them to babble. When you finish answering the question, quietly tolerate the silence and wait. No more than 15 seconds will pass before the interviewer asks the next question, and you will demonstrate your self-confidence, professional demeanor, poise, and ability to handle pressure.

There are specific situations intended to put you in the hot seat for the entire interview. Although these are more rare today, let me describe two scenarios and give you ideas on how to handle each of them. The first requires two or three interviewers. They begin by rapidly firing questions, allowing little if any time to answer one question before the next one is thrown at you. The IRS has often used this style when interviewing for collectors, auditors, and agents. The correct response is to say, "Just a minute here. I do want to answer your questions, so let's start with Tom first and once I've answered his question, then I'll answer George's. Tom, could you repeat your question, please?" Regaining control is the only way to not be disqualified as a potential candidate.

The second example rarely happens, but just might. The interviewer walks into the room, sits down, and glares at you. He says, "You don't know anything," as he crumples your resumé into a ball and throws it on the floor. He waits for your reaction. Commonly, people feel fear, anger, and disgust. This person is demanding and intimidating because he feels the job will require you to deal with demanding people. An appropriate response would be: "There is a lot I can learn from you." And see where this leads. Do your best to listen. Demonstrate that you are easy to train, eager to learn. Play to the person's ego. Then once you leave, seriously evaluate if this is a good work environment for you. The dictator will probably use intimidation on the job. This style should raise a serious concern for you about whether you really want to work for this person and his organization.

Breakfast/Lunch/Dinner Interviews

Meals often provide a more relaxed atmosphere, and candidates often chat, saying things that hurt their candidacy. This is an interview—you are not speaking off the record; *all ears are listening to you*. Remain in your role and answer each question accordingly. More lengthy answers are okay, but never monopolize the conversation. Be aware of the interviewer's desire to learn about the *real* you. He or she also watches your restaurant etiquette. Allow the interviewer to pay for the meal. Select an entrée that is easy to eat, not spaghetti or lobster or messy finger foods. Focus on the conversation and be cordial. I recommend you never drink. This is a job interview. If you must drink, nurse something very slowly, leaving it half touched. You need to remain sharp.

These meetings often try to uncover personality traits, outside interests, and personal information. Are you a good conversationalist? Would you interact well at company functions or client meetings? What are your personal circumstances? Are you single? Married? Do you have children? Are you divorced? Do you have time-consuming sports or hobbies?

To control this meeting, ask a lot of questions about the company, the duties of the job, and immediate challenges. A good conversation question is to ask the interviewer how he or she likes the company and why it's a good place to work. Throughout this interview, continually sell yourself and your ability to do the job.

Video or Video Conferencing Interview

These are rare situations, but it has happened to a couple of my clients and it might happen to you. In one situation, the company videotapes the entire process. Often this is to "show" management back at headquarters the candidates and eliminate the expense of flying you to that location. Trainers and sales personnel are most likely to be asked to be videotaped. Often a short presentation is required from you as part of this process. You are almost always told in advance about this type of format. Here are some guidelines:

- Ask in advance all the details about this format. Whom is it for? Where will the camera be? How long will the interview be? Are there any special presentations you will be asked to make? Don't expect the interviewer to volunteer much, so ask and call back a second time if you need more clarification.
- Practice using a video camera to record a role-playing session. Your movements and nervous actions are exaggerated on video. Watch for your nonverbal clues and facial expressions.
- Focus totally on the interviewer and forget the camera. Staring into the camera will just make you nervous and cause you to make mistakes.
- Your poise and self-confidence are being assessed here. Be sure to exude these traits.
- Smile often—when the tape is viewed, you will come across as a warmer, more likable person.

Video conferencing is another interview format you may encounter. One of my clients in Seattle was interviewed for a federal job in Washington, D.C. through this medium. She was an accountant and a very introverted person, and this process really intimidated her until we worked together. She did land the job. These tips made a big difference for her and will help you if you face the same situation.

- Ask about the details of how the process will work. Arrive a few minutes ahead of schedule to get comfortable with the setup. Usually it's your potential boss on the other end.
- Try to pretend this is face-to-face and not a TV monitor.
- Smile, and show enthusiasm to build rapport.
- Avoid staring directly into the camera as it'll make you nervous. Ask where the best place to look is so the interviewer on the other end can see your face, your warm smile, and not a profile or just hair.
- Relax and rely on your preparation; use your 5 Point Agenda, your 60 Second Sell, and good work examples, and keep your answers under 60 seconds—with video conferencing, shorter answers are better.

Testing Interview

Many companies hire outside consultants to help them develop a profile and determine each candidate's true skills, abilities, and personality traits. The consultants or HR personnel ask you to take a test, or several for that matter. They can be: a math quiz, a personality test (Myers-Briggs is commonly used), a computer usage test having you demonstrate your skill in using Word or Excel, an in-box test, a manager test with case study problems to solve, a correspondence test where you are given a client/customer or employee letter to write a short response to, and so on. These tests can be short or last a day or two. They can make most candidates nervous—very nervous, since the pressure's on to perform well. Do your best and ask for clear directions. No one ever gets a perfect score on two days of assessment. But employers are seeking to validate your strengths and uncover weaknesses, so be careful and thorough; read directions twice and follow them exactly. Be sure to proofread answers and pay attention to proper spelling and grammar.

One client sailed through day one of the personality test and an afternoon of replying to videotaped job problems (an angry customer, an employee squabble, a project with a deadline, and missing work problems). It was the in-box procedure he felt he didn't do well on. Indeed he hadn't, with the consultant's report labeling him disorganized. His dream job slipping away, he wrote his potential boss a detailed letter explaining how he organized his last complex job and projects. The employer questioned the true accuracy of the testing (as hiring managers often do) and hired this client, who's proved to be one of the best managers in the company.

Fly-In/Relocation Interview

Usually you've had a screening interview prior to the company's deciding that it will fly you in for the next interview. Whenever possible, try to arrive the day before the actual interview. Many candidates have been nervous wrecks when they arrived late, or just minutes before the interview was to start, because of late flights and poor directions. These interviews often require a relocation, though occasionally it's just the "head office" wanting to see you before giving you the job in the region where you live. Relocation is a major decision, so think it through and get on the Web and research the city, tourist attractions, cost of living, and quality of life.

A common mistake is to arrive at these interviews too overconfident, thinking, "They must really like me if they are covering all the costs to see me." Never assume the job is yours or that the interview is an expenses-paid vacation. These attitudes often lead to losing the position.

Some tips to remember:

- Know in advance who'll pay for expenses; typically, the company does. Be leery of companies that want you to cover all the costs and say they'll "reimburse" you. It could take months to get the money if you ever get it at all.
- Ask the company to make the hotel reservation, keeping convenience to the company's location as the first priority.
- Place your interview outfit and all your job search materials in carry-on luggage. You can't afford the embarrassment that lost luggage causes.
- It's usually acceptable to ask to stay on a day or two to check out the area. You might inquire if someone from the company could show you around. Look at apartments and houses in nice areas and get prices to have a more realistic idea of what it costs to live in the area.
- Watch expenses. Now is not the time to treat friends or order steak and lobster with expensive wine, running up high expense bills.

- Taxis are often an easier way for you to get around, especially in cities like L.A. or D.C., where traffic is bad even when it's not rush hour. If you rent a car, get a map and clear directions—always stop and ask if you are lost.
- Be safe. If you ever feel that the hotel is in a high-crime or unsafe area—move. Single women need to exercise caution, especially going anywhere in a new city alone at night.
- Show interest in both the city and the job. One candidate, interviewing at a prestigious law firm, lost the job when a partner asked, "So are you ready to leave San Francisco and move to Boston?" Her "I'm not sure" caused him to offer a more interested and committed candidate the job. Use this trip to really evaluate: Can I live here? Would I like it? Would my family? Will it fast-track my career? Is it a good job? Does it pay well enough so I maintain or improve my standard of living?

Bizarre Interview

Over the years, I've heard of some very strange things that have happened on interviews, such as:

- "Forget the interview, let's go out on a date," or worse, being propositioned
- Throwing a football at you as you walk through the door—if you catch it, you get hired
- Yelling obscenities at you
- Putting you in a dark closet for two hours to see what you'll do

The list goes on. Yes, these employers must have a reason for such behavior, but my question to you is this: *Why would you ever want to work for them?*

If a red flag goes up inside your head when a potential employer gets bizarre, heed the warning and look elsewhere for the job of your dreams.

Negotiation Interview

The job offer has been made. You're now in control. The employer has changed hats and eagerly attempts to get you to join his team. Use this time to learn about the politics, the company's goals, and the role your position and decisions will play in the global scheme of the company. Ask about promotional tracks and training opportunities. Ask to meet your potential staff, and if you have not met the person who would be your boss, insist on it before you accept. You should now learn all about their benefits and decide on an agreeable salary.

This interview can be vital to your assessment of the corporate culture. Often people take the job when it is offered by phone. They start, and within a week they know they've made a terrible mistake. Often, a negotiation interview would have revealed potential conflicts, such as changes in benefits, or job duties different from those that were mentioned at the first interview. One client was promised a necessary and highly desirable training program. At the negotiation interview that promise was changed: the training would be offered six months or so down the line. That training was vital to her success. When a few other things changed also, she passed on the job.

There may be reasons to refuse a job. Ask, "Are there any problems, situations, or reasons that exist that could dissuade me from taking this job?" Never underestimate intense, political conflicts between employees you will manage. Get the facts and think the situation through thoroughly. Determine the time, energy, and upper-management agenda necessary to solve or continue this often emotionally draining situation.

Lastly, ask if there was an internal candidate who did not get this job. Will you supervise that person? How will he or she react to you? Be concerned about how that candidate's workmates will interact and treat you. Be careful—these situations can often sabotage your ability to succeed in the new position.

Gather your facts, insights, and impressions during this time. Properly utilized, this interview allows you to select an organization where you really can leave each day saying, "I love my job."

*Act as if it were impossible to fail
and you never will.*

Chapter 10

Pitfalls to Avoid

Part of our strategy for a successful interview is to have you avoid mistakes that many people often make. The 20 common errors you'll want to avoid are:

1. Being Late

Many employers feel that if you're late for the interview, you may never show up on time for your job. Need I say more? Get the directions, know how to get there, and give yourself more than enough time so that you can arrive early. Wait, collect your thoughts, and then open the employer's door about five minutes early.

2. Inappropriate Attire

Most people simply don't think about their appearance. They don't realize the importance of that first few seconds, when they meet the employer for the first time. The employer looks at you and, based on your appearance, decides whether or not you would fit in his organization. He decides not to hire you based on the way you're dressed and your personal hygiene. Whether you like it or not, it's human nature and it happens every day. The employer's immediate decision is based on whether you would be an appropriate person to *represent* the company. Remember, *you want to get the job*. The interview is not the time to express your creative personality. Many people lose jobs because of their wild clothes, earrings, mismatched colors, greasy hair, dirty nails, and sloppiness. Put your best foot forward. After all, it is important that the interview *not* end the moment the interviewer sees you.

Appearance is crucial for people who are in high-visibility positions. You'd be surprised at some of the things I've seen people wear to interview—gaudy makeup, mini-miniskirts, old-fashioned suits two sizes too small. The list is endless. Dress well and be conservative even in today's more casual work environment. I recommend that men wear business suits; navy blue and dark gray have tested well. A white shirt is the best choice. Select a very conservative tie. For women, a business suit, a business coat dress, or a jacket over a skirt are appropriate. I recommend you not wear pants. You probably know what colors look best on you, but navy blue is always a safe color for an interview suit. Something stylish, but conservative, never sexy.

Designate an interview outfit that you know is clean, fits well, and can be worn to any interview on last-minute notice. Be sure your outfit makes a positive impression on people. A good way to test out an outfit is to wear it to a meeting, then ask people to comment about your outfit and see what kind of reaction you get. This test will give you the feedback to know whether or not it's an outfit you should wear to an interview. Large department stores have personal shoppers; they can also assist you in getting a professional outfit. But don't try to get too trendy. Most organizations like a conservative look.

3. No Market Research

It's amazing to me how many people go to a job interview with no information about the company, no thought about the job that they'll be doing, and no idea as to how they're going to relate their skills to the company's needs. The more inside information you can get, the more accurately you're going to be able to phrase your answers to demonstrate how your skills will fill the employer's needs. This is effective self-marketing. Spend the time to call contacts, read company literature, and go on the Internet to learn as much as possible about the employer's needs to help direct you in properly answering the interviewer's questions. It's imperative to your success. Many a candidate has not been hired because he appeared clueless about the company and meeting its needs.

4. Assume Your Resumé Will Get You the Job

Do you believe that the employer diligently, and with a microscope, went through your resumé and absorbed every single fact there? In reality, hiring managers often have glanced at the resumé when they offered you an interview, and have not looked at it again until the second you're in front of them. Secondly, employers know that good resumés can be purchased. In fact, it's best to assume your resumé will not get you the job. You will be selling your skills throughout the entire interview. Don't say, "Oh, well it's in my resumé." Assume they *haven't read* your resumé and say, "I've got 10 years of experience in the graphic design field."

5. Believe That the Person with the Best Education, Skills, and Experience Will Get the Job

This is not the case based on my experience as a hiring employer, and on discussions with numerous other employers. Sometimes the person that has the best experience, the best skills, and the best education doesn't feel like she'd fit into the organization. She just doesn't have the right personality or a cooperative attitude. Also, employers may become concerned that the candidate is overqualified and will leave too quickly. Whatever the reason, don't assume that top credentials are all it takes to get hired.

6. Fail to Prepare

This is a fatal error. I can't stress enough how important it is that you prepare prior to the interview. Write out answers to prospective questions. Analyze and prepare your 5 Point Agenda. Memorize your 60 Second Sell. Practice interview questions using a role-playing situation. Try a tape recorder or get feedback from another person. Advanced preparation makes you feel and sound confident about your abilities to do the job. It's crucial to your success.

7. Believe the Interviewer Is an Expert

This is a myth. Most managers hire only their own staff. Very few are skillfully trained in techniques on how to conduct an interview. Those that receive any training often just get instructions on which questions are legal to ask. Don't assume that they'll know the direction the interview needs to go. Sometimes it's to your advantage to direct the conversation to effectively make your points.

8. Fail to Inspire Confidence

Interviews are not the time to be humble and meek. If you don't express competency and confidence that you can do the job, the employer will recognize that you probably *can't* do the job. Eye contact, a smile, and some enthusiasm in your voice are good covers for any nervousness you feel inside. Many employers have told me during reference checks, "She's really quite good at the job—it's too bad she interviews so poorly." Practice, practice, practice and you will improve.

9. Fail to Demonstrate Skills

Many people will sit through the interview, but they don't clearly tell the employer the skills that they'd bring to the job. They're quiet; their answers may be very general or very vague. Employers don't hire for vague generalities. They hire for specifics. Specific skills, past experience, examples of how you have done that kind of work before. Specifics are what employers make decisions to hire on. Be sure to be detailed, but concise, whenever you answer.

10. Appear Desperate or Highly Stressed Out

An unfortunate reality of hiring is that people are desperate. When you're an employer, interviewing with somebody whose desperation keeps coming through often makes you feel sorry for the person, but you don't hire him. I've had many employers tell me, "You know, I really felt sorry for him," but when I asked, "Well, did you hire him?" they all said, "Well no, I didn't." The desperation turns them off. They're afraid that person doesn't want their particular job, he just wants *any* job. And to the employer, you wanting *their* job is what's most important. You want to appear as if there are other opportunities on your horizon. You may have to act; maybe you *are* desperate. But if you convey that desperation to the employer in the interview, it can hurt your chances of getting hired.

11. Mishandle Supplemental Questions or Tests

Some employers will ask you to fill out additional questionnaires or take a test during the hiring process. These must be taken seriously, so try to gather as much information as possible in advance to prepare thoroughly. Ask the organization for the specific details on exactly what the tests or written supplemental questions will be about. Don't guess, *know*. Be sure to think carefully and to follow directions for all written answers. Proofread and be as careful as possible.

I've seen employers give equipment-stimulation tests, typing tests, computer tests, written exams, personality tests, problems to solve, materials to proofread, work to analyze and prioritize, plus other tasks to determine your hireability. Learn as much as you can and practice in advance. The day of the interview, practice again, then do your best. Most errors come from making yourself too nervous, putting an exorbitant amount of pressure on yourself, or being unprepared. Some employers may want you to submit to a drug test. Do so. Your refusal will eliminate you as a candidate. If you take prescription medicine, inform the person conducting the test to document the prescription.

12. Believe That the Most Important Time Is the Last Five Minutes

Actually, the most important time is the first 60 seconds, when the interviewer at least makes the decision that she's going to listen to you. Then take every opportunity to demonstrate your skills and your abilities with proven examples of work you've done in the past. In reality, using *all* the time well is most important.

13. Think That References Are All Created Equal

They are not. Some individuals, especially those who have previously worked with you, can aid you in being offered a position. Other times, they can actually deter an employer from hiring you. When choosing references, consider testing them out to learn exactly what they will say about you. Ask a friend to call and get a reference on you. Have that person report back. One client reported that her assistant discussed how the assistant had really organized the office himself and the client came off in a less than favorable light. Needless to say, she dropped that name from her reference list.

Obtain permission from a reference in advance. Help them to be a good reference by writing them a letter and nicely reminding them about the experiences and abilities you'd like them to discuss. This letter often helps refresh their memories if it's been a while since you've worked together.

Under no circumstances use a boss who will say negative things. Find someone else who can talk about your strengths and contributions even if you were fired. After all, you select your references, so choose those names carefully. Be sure to check that all references' information—titles, addresses, phone numbers—is correct so that the employer doesn't find the people on your list are "no longer here."

14. Not Being the Ideal Worker

Employers want workers willing to be adaptable, to learn new skills, and to take on new tasks as needed. All jobs undergo change in some form or another. Demonstrate that you love to learn and are willing to do whatever is needed to help the department and company achieve its goals now and in the future.

15. Lying on the Resumé or Application

Nearly one-third of all job applicants have been caught lying about their education. Employers often check, so never misrepresent yourself—firing is almost always the result. Fudging on salary when asked to state "last salary" on an application is also lying and will not be validated when your employer is called and asked, "Can you verify Mary Brown's salary was $41,500?" You'll be in trouble if the answer is no. (Incidentally, all employers can do is validate—they won't reveal a salary figure when asked.) The best approach is to leave the salary request blank. Strive to state things in a positive manner but do so honestly, with integrity, expecting that the employer will check.

16. Appear Uninterested in the Job

Fear and intimidation often keep people from relaxing and performing well in an interview. They resort to a monotone voice that makes them seem to lack any enthusiasm for the job. Employers want you to *want* their job. Be friendly, smile, and ask good questions (see chapter 5 for help). If you don't act interested, the employer will hire someone else who does.

17. Bragging

Selling yourself effectively means giving examples that substantiate your claims. Bragging often comes from weak candidates thinking they can snow the interviewer. You must be prepared to demonstrate *the results* of your sales ability, leadership, or whatever else you claim to be outstanding in. Results, specifics, and examples with substance are what will really influence an employer.

18. Give Lengthy Answers

An interviewer's attention span will fade quickly, so don't bore him to death. One CFO commented after an interview with a potential vice president, "Wow, could you imagine that guy in a meeting? He'd never get to the point and we'd be there all day," referring to an applicant's 20-minute response to a question.

Best approach—keep the conversation moving by answering questions in less than 60 seconds.

19. Inability to Tolerate Pauses or Silence

The interviewer does not expect or need you to speak every second. When you finish answering a question, just *tolerate* the silence while he or she absorbs your answer, takes notes, or formulates the next question. Don't babble on and on—

you often appear nervous (you are) and come across as a poor communicator to the interviewer. Be concise and thorough, but never take more than a minute with your response.

20. Think Your Major Goal Is to Get the Job

Really? I thought your major goal is to find out about the job, to learn what the company's needs are, and to examine and determine if your skills and abilities fit their needs. Would this be a good marriage? Uniting your skills and abilities, their jobs needs, and bringing you both together? That's really what you're looking for. During the interview you are investigating them just as they are investigating you. Realize it's an exchange from which both of you will decide if this is a possible fit and a good job for you. Use the time to gather decision-making information for yourself to aid you in determining whether this is a position in which you'll be able to contribute, be productive, and enjoy going to work.

*A*lways do your best.

It is your constant effort

to be first-class

in everything you attempt

that will make you conquer

the heights of excellence and success.

Chapter 11

The Spotlight Is on You

In every interview you are an actor. Your role is the job seeker. Just as Hollywood's top stars practice and prepare, so will you. Every actor knows that spoken words are enhanced by body language, facial expressions, voice intonations, and props. When the job interview's spotlight shines on you, you begin a one-time-only performance. So make your words, body language, and voice work to aid you in landing the job.

Dealing with Nervousness

Important events where we are judged and need to perform well can make anyone nervous. A little nervousness can actually help you be sharp and on your toes, and improve your performance. A heart-thumping, face-twitching, voice-quivering nervousness will reflect poorly on you and the strong, self-confident, "I can solve your problems" impression you are trying to make. Try these techniques to lessen your nervousness.

Technique 1

Visualize success. See yourself smiling and happy. In your mind, create a picture of the employer's eyes glued to you, hanging on every word. Hear her say, "I want you for the job." Believe that you will be successful, liked, and wanted in this encounter. Your state of mind directly impacts your performance. Focus only on confidence-building thoughts.

Technique 2

Listen to a motivational tape shortly before the interview. The confidence- and morale-boosting words will give you needed moral support and decrease your apprehensions.

Technique 3

Rid your body of nervous tension. Just before you go into the interview find a private spot outside or in the rest room, and shake each leg. Then shake both arms and hands. The physical exercise releases the tension that has built up, and relaxes you.

Technique 4

Take deep breaths. As your hand reaches for the door, take a couple of deep breaths, slowly breathing in and out. Think of a calm and beautifully peaceful scene to help you relax a bit.

All four techniques will help to decrease your nervousness. And practice makes perfect. All the preparation creating answers, and your 60 Second Sell, should reassure you that you are prepared and will do your best.

What to Bring

The night before the interview pack up what you need to bring. Always have extra resumés—yes, they do lose them and misplace them. Bring your list of references. Be sure all addresses and phone numbers are current and accurate. Include any work samples and the list of questions you intend to ask. Carry your research, the list of those questions you want answered, your 5 Point Agenda, and your 60 Second Sell. You'll want to review all this preparation an hour or two before entering the interview to keep the ideas fresh in your mind. Include a notepad and pen in case you need them.

Decide if you will carry a briefcase or a simple leather-bound notebook holder into the interview. Organize your materials, and you are ready to go. Be careful not to have too many things—briefcase, notepad binder, materials, purse—all in your hands. Combine and compact into one easily carried piece, two maximum.

First Impressions

First impressions are difficult to change. Before you even say hello, the employer's mind is evaluating attire, hygiene, and style, formulating an opinion, since what you wear sends powerful signals. They must be positive or these could eliminate your chances of getting the job. Select a suit that is conservative, but modern. Be certain it is clean and fits well, and pay careful attention to the details. Smile at everyone you meet. As you introduce yourself to the receptionist, smile and take a moment to ask her name. Be sure to add that you are glad to meet her. When the interviewer approaches, stand, smile, and offer a firm handshake. Nothing creates a poorer impression than a weak couple-of-fingers shake. Start out exuding confidence; the smile and firm handshake are key.

Nonverbal Clues

Employers evaluate what they hear, while giving credence to what they see. Nervous gestures such as playing with your hair or tapping your fingers can absorb their attention. Nervous job hunters then compensate by crossing their arms, a gesture that radiates a closed, unapproachable, "Stay away from me" message. To demonstrate that you are relaxed and confident, sit with your hands on your lap, or rest them open on the table if one is in front of you. Equally acceptable is to open your notepad and have a pen to hold.

Your movements, gestures, posture, and facial expressions are an important part of your overall performance. A sincere smile sends a warm, confident message. Eye contact is one of the important things employers notice about you. It is crucial and conveys that your message is believable. We all get suspicious of a person who focuses his eyes on the floor, to the side, but rarely on us. Practice until it is second nature to look *at* the person when answering a question.

Your face can reflect so many expressions—humor, confidence, seriousness, concern, enthusiasm—all of which add depth and meaning to your words. Be sure to not sit there stoically, with a blank face. So often you fail to appear "real" and come across boring and dull. If you sit rigid, upright, or frozen you communicate anxiety and insincerity. Likewise, slouching projects cowardliness, insecurity, less competence. Sit up tall, but lean forward from time to time to make your point and draw in your listener.

Use vocal intonations to make your point. Pauses, soft tones, and louder tones all add interest to a conversation. One department head commented that she listens to applicants' tone. If they are long-winded, monotonic, and boring, she eliminates them. After all, she is the one who will constantly be listening to them in meetings. She, like many employers, wants someone confident, human, more personable. This does not mean loud and boisterous. Quiet introverts often excel in interviews because they project a quiet, confident self. Be yourself, be natural, but use these nonverbal techniques to project a more appealing image to the employer.

Support Documentation

Proof. Every employer loves to see proof that you can do his job. Just as a graphic designer never interviews without a portfolio holding samples of her work, you need to bring samples that demonstrate your abilities to do the job.

Proof can be a form you have created that sped up production, a spreadsheet that is an efficient tracking system, articles you have written, materials you have created, brochures that list you as a panelist or speaker. Bring anything that clearly demonstrates how you have done the job before. Remember, a picture, or in this case, a paper, journal, flyer, etc., is worth a thousand words.

Field Knowledge

An employer often dreads all the time necessary to teach a person trying to change careers about the new field. To prevent this from becoming a hiring obstacle, especially if you are trying to change fields, be self-taught. Read books and articles on the new field you want to enter. Talk with successful people who hold jobs similar to the one you want. Learn the field's jargon, the future trends, the impact these trends might have. Acquire the needed background to eliminate the employer's concern that you know *nothing* about this field.

For job hunters trying to remain in their field, read up on trends, new changes, and current problems, so as to be nimble and able to discuss your position and the field in which the work is done. Learn the field's needs, and how you fill those needs. Become well versed in the potential company's product, services, and operations. If you educate yourself before the interview, you can make a very appealing package and cross over into new and very different, complex fields or companies. Never go to the interview without doing this important homework. Every applicant must also stress his interest in the field, and the desire to stay up on changes and learn new skills to better perform the job.

60 Second Work Example

Clearly communicating by using an example can paint a picture that allows the employer to see you doing similar tasks, successfully, for her. Predetermined work examples are a very effective part of the tools you bring to the meeting. You'll never flounder and search for an example. Preselection allows you to slowly sift through your background and extract the right situation to make your point. Prepare examples that demonstrate each component in your 5 Point Agenda. Prepare examples that deal with problem solving, supervisory style, your teamwork ability, and planning and organization skills, especially if your job deals with projects and deadlines. These examples or stories need to be introduced, told, then summarized in no more than 60 seconds. Advance preparation allows you to use these examples to answer questions appropriately.

If you are asked a question about dealing with employee performance or problem solving, you could try an example like this: "Solving problems is an important part of my work. At Northwest Hospital I had a staff person who was overwhelmed with her regular workload and trying to learn our new software. Everything was getting behind. I sat her down and we talked about the problem. Laura found it very hard to concentrate with any distractions as she applied what she'd been taught in the computer training class. We decided that Laura could spend one hour each day for two weeks with her door closed and her phone forwarded to voice mail. We determined specific goals she needed to reach that were necessary for her to master the new software so she could get the department back up to speed. I encouraged her daily, and she did make the needed progress. In fact, she surpassed all my expectations and within two months really improved our paper-flow productivity with her new skills. I think it was the effort I made getting her input and help in finding an acceptable solution that encouraged and motivated her to try harder." When you offer specific details you make the employer think, "Yes, that's what we need." Using examples, you'll go a long way toward being hired.

Incorporate Transferable Skills

Many of your abilities are skills that are valuable from one employer to another. These "transferable skills" build a fuller picture for the employer to consider.

You possess many skills that you fail to recognize but that an employer will see as necessary and important. At the top of most employers' lists are *computer skills*—highly valued from one employer to another. Here are other skill areas to consider. Select those that are important in doing the employer's job well and incorporate them into your answers and examples.

- **Managerial Skills.** Set goals, see the big picture, solve problems, handle details, plan projects, analyze, find resources, work well with others, obtain maximum productivity from others, gain cooperation, implement changes, supervise others, plan workflow, mediate staff conflicts, delegate, think globally.
- **Organizational/Planning Skills.** Structure events, coordinate people and details, organize tracking or filing systems, set timelines, forecast, determine priorities, manage all aspects of large or multiple projects, develop alternatives, determine resources, solve problems, see the big picture and all the interacting components too, pay attention to the tiniest details, gather support and cooperation from others.
- **Communication Skills.** Exchange ideas, use probing questions to determine needs of others, sell products/services/ideas, persuade others to do what you want, use humor, tell stories, entertain others, write messages that clearly get across your meaning, teach or train, make impassioned pleas, edit comprehensive reports/proposals, express creativity, use vocabulary/grammar/language skills effectively, edit reports/publications, make speeches.
- **Leadership Skills.** Lead, motivate others, cause change, make decisions, be a visionary, forecast,

recognize opportunities, praise others, direct projects and individuals.

- **Customer Service Skills.** Meeting client/customer needs, troubleshooting, resourceful problem solving, courteous manner, listening, helpful attitude.
- **Financial Skills.** Budgets, cost spreadsheets, price comparisons, negotiate better deals, notice cost-cutting or profit-making opportunities, cash management, using charts/graphs to make points, stretching a dollar, financial analysis.
- **Analytical Skills.** Research, analyze data, interpret results, organize large volumes of information, evaluate options considering pros/cons and consequences, design efficient systems, collect and process information in user-friendly form, diagnose problems, determine workable solutions, seek more efficient procedures, produce technical reports/surveys or questionnaires, investigate, make new discoveries, implement new systems, test new ideas/processes/procedures/systems.
- **Interpersonal Skills.** Counseling, negotiations, listening, empathy, sensitivity to others, rapport builder, deal effectively with conflicts, social interacter, help others, share ideas, solve problems, adviser, mediator, bring people together.

Handling Small Employers

In the next decade, according to the Department of Labor, job growth will increase by the greatest degree with small employers, particularly organizations with fewer than 100 people. This presents a dilemma to you, since often very little information about the employer is available prior to the interview. To aid you in your preparation, try to obtain as much information from the person who arranges the interview or try someone else in the office. Call and ask a few questions. If you get, "Oh, they'll cover that," you'll need to use your best guess and prepare. As you start the interview, if you employ this technique, you can gain the necessary information and reorganize your answers to address their spoken needs. Simply say, "Mr. Employer, *before we get started*, could you tell me in more detail about the day-to-day responsibilities?" Then ask, "What do you consider the priorities? Is there any special training or experience you're seeking?" Be sure to use the "before we get started" phrase—it allows you to gain insight, and the employer believes he hasn't begun yet even though this information will help you frame your answers.

From those few questions, you've learned the important ingredients this employer desires. You can address his needs by quickly editing your 60 Second Sell. You may need to adapt quickly, but you've gotten the insights and can now stress your strengths to meet his needs, while most other candidates will be operating blind.

Listen

Hear their questions, *hear* their needs, *hear* their expectations. If you listen carefully, employers often reveal everything you need to know.

Often job hunters just don't listen. It is frustrating to the interviewer to ask questions that never get answered. So listen closely. Many employers reveal their "hidden agendas," those few things that really influence their decision, if you listen closely to the questions they ask and the information they offer. I recently interviewed four people in order to hire a program coordinator. I told each candidate that computer skills were important. One person emphasized her organizational abilities, another her attention to detail and willingness to do whatever was asked. A third repeatedly discussed her computer abilities but never addressed the fact that my company was using different software. The gentleman I hired spoke about his computer abilities and brought sample flyers, documents, and even a newsletter he'd done. He met my most important criterion—good computer skills. The others never heard me. As the potential employer, I told them, but they didn't listen. If they had, they might have been the one who got the job. Instead, he did!

The only people who fail
are those who do not try.
All your dreams can come true
if you have the courage to pursue them.
The bigger you dream
the more you will achieve.

Chapter 12

The Convincing Close

Most employers use some sort of rating system at the end of an interview. Some may just jot down notes; others use a comprehensive evaluation form. With this in mind, how you end the interview will be a vital component in securing the job offer.

Be Memorable—End with Your 60 Second Sell

Most seasoned interviewers will tell you that it is easy to forget a person 60 seconds after she runs out the door. You can often sit back at the end of the day, look at the resumés, and wonder who was who.

Using the 60 Second Sell and the 5 Point Agenda ensures repetition of your major strengths. Creating examples that demonstrates these strengths and effectively answering questions in less than 60 seconds will reinforce your abilities and your desire to do the job. Using your 60 Second Sell as you are ending the interview will leave the employer with those few thoughts to ponder as she fills out her evaluation form, remembering your five most marketable skills to meet her company's needs and do the job.

The end has come; the employer has asked all her questions, and you've followed with yours. You've learned about the next stage and when the company will be making a decision. Just before you get up to leave, close with your 60 Second Sell. Be sure to incorporate any major point that you learned from the employer during the interview, replacing one of the original five points with a new one to hit upon the organization's need. Here's how one client won the job:

"Thank you for the opportunity to meet with you and learn about your needs for an executive director. I believe my 13 years in association management, assisting associations in their development and growth, would be an asset to you. It sounds as if I'd be able to put to use all the event planning and the media contacts I've developed to create very profitable events, obtaining the publicity and corporate sponsors that ensure high attendance. I believe the addition of seminars and workshops would be a new revenue source for you, as it was for my last employer. Finally, I think my resourcefulness to be innovative, maximize the use of volunteers, and work with restricted budgets would be very beneficial in achieving your goals. I believe I would make some very valuable contributions if I joined your team. Thank you again for this meeting and your interest."

Format the close to directly apply your abilities to what the employer has revealed about the position. Once said, stand, shake hands, and leave.

Employer Rating Chart

As soon as the door closes, the employer takes notes. She decides whether or not you are someone she could work with. Below is a typical ratings report an employer might complete after each interview. Note that this employer uses facts and impressions she's gathered during the interview process. First the determination—*can you do the job*—evaluating technical competency, noting weaknesses and strengths. Skill areas are examined; job knowledge, communication skills, managerial style, organizational/planning problem-solving and decision-making abilities are rated. A decision is made about whether you are a potential candidate to be hired for the job. See the chart on pages 162 and 163.

Postinterview Assessment

Immediately after the interview, find a spot to sit down and write out your assessment of the employer and the position. This will help you to improve your interviews in the future and to evaluate the employer's needs for future interviews if the process continues; also, note any special problems or tough questions to practice answering in the future. Jot down these thoughts:

- Describe job duties
- Impression of the potential workplace
- Impression of future boss
- Concerns or weak areas you might have in performing this job
- Training time to get up to speed
- Unanswered questions or concerns you'll need further clarification on
- Tough questions you found hard to answer
- Rate your performance
- Note any areas where you might try to improve
- Are you interested in this job? Company?

Interview Evaluation

Name: _____

Position: _____

Technical competency:
Candidate's strongest skills are:

1. _____
2. _____
3. _____

Compared to our job needs, these strengths are:
__ Not important   __ Somewhat Important   __ Important

Previous job performance of technical skills:
__ Poor __ Below average __ Adequate __ Good __ Excellent

Weakness or areas of concern: _____

_____

Overall job knowledge:
__ Poor __ Below average __ Adequate __ Good __ Excellent

Oral communication skills:
__ Poor __ Below average __ Adequate __ Good __ Excellent

Written communication skills:
__ Poor __ Below average __ Adequate __ Good __ Excellent

Organizational/planning abilities:
__ Poor __ Below average __ Adequate __ Good __ Excellent

Managerial skills:
Describe candidate's supervisory style: _____

_____

_____

Rate style in relation to managing employees who will report to this person:
__ Poor __ Below average __ Adequate __ Good __ Excellent

Computer skills:
Hardware experience: _____
Software experience: _____
Training needed: _____

Decision-making experience:
__ Poor __ Below average __ Adequate __ Good __ Excellent

Interpersonal/customer skills:
__ Poor __ Below average __ Adequate __ Good __ Excellent

Analytical abilities:
__ Poor __ Below average __ Adequate __ Good __ Excellent

Work ethic:
__ Poor __ Below average __ Adequate __ Good __ Excellent

Personality:
Describe: _____
_____

Asset for the job:
__ No __ Yes __ Most definitely
Comments: _____
_____

Hiring rating:
__ Definitely not __ Adequate with some reservations
__ Possible hire __ Definitely hire
Explanation: _____
_____

Signature: _____
Date: _____

Thank You Notes

Employers can be influenced once you have left the room. A thank-you note that arrives can often reaffirm that they have made the right choice. The note can tip the hand in your favor if the choice is between you and someone else. The employer believes a person who really wants the job is likely to perform better on the job. Your note could be on a note card with the words "Thank You" printed in a professional, businesslike style (these are available in the local drugstore or card shop). Or choose plain expensive note card stationery that looks professional and expensive. Jot down a few lines, thanking the employer for the opportunity and reiterating a strength or two you would bring as a "valuable contributor to their team." Often, seminar students object, saying, "Shouldn't I type a letter?" Typed letters do not have the same impact. Sometimes they are opened by an assistant and not seen by the employer. Other times, they are only glanced at. The note—handwritten (print if your writing is not legible)—is a *personal* communication. Demonstrate the extra effort you put into your work. It certainly won't negatively impact your chances. It's important to mention that most candidates *do not* send thank-you notes. Here again is the chance to move to the top and be reevaluated. Notes must be mailed within 24 hours, preferably the same day as the interview if timing allows.

How to Remain a Viable Candidate
When Someone Else Gets the Job

Up to 15% of all new hires do not work out within the first two months. The reasons vary—perhaps the candidate continued interviewing and got a better offer, or his performance and personality did not fit the employer's needs.

One candidate accepted a position for a top management position. Relocation was involved, so the employer agreed to wait eight weeks for the candidate to start. On the night before he was scheduled to start, a fax arrived saying the person had changed his mind and wasn't coming.

There are times when *follow-up can win you the job.* Here's what to do:

1. Call to verify that the employer selected another candidate. Reiterate that you are still interested in the job if the person doesn't work out, and ask the employer to reconsider you if that should happen. A few of my clients ended up with the job simply because they did this and made it easy for the employer to call them again. Don't burden the employer with questions on what you did wrong—he is not likely to honestly share that information. And never argue or get defensive. The employer will hire the person he feels is best suited for the job. A great technique many clients have had success using is to inquire whether the company has any other available positions that you might qualify for. If so, secure the name of the hiring manager and contact that person at once. It's also a good idea to ask, "I'm sorry it didn't work out, Bill; by chance do you know of any other companies looking for a (use the job title you interviewed for) like me?" This has led savvy job hunters to their next new position.

2. Check back in four to six weeks to see if the person is working out. If he isn't, the employer will be very glad to hear from you.

3. When you are not the first choice, ask about the other person's skill and experience with a couple of probing questions. "I understand the person had more experience— in what areas?" Asking nicely in a *"help me out so I'll improve"*

approach can allow you to see where your answers and responses need work in the future. If you feel the employer missed some important aspect of your background you can add, "I recognize that I was a little nervous during the interview and probably didn't communicate to you very well my experience in ———" (you fill in the blank). Then offer solid examples of this experience. If the employer shows interest, ask to meet with him again—anytime, anyplace. This has helped people obtain a second interview after HR eliminated them.

4. Forget your pride. Pride does not pay your bills. Perhaps you didn't get the initial offer because you didn't sell yourself as effectively as you could have. Whether you are second, third, or fifth choice does not matter if in the end you're the one who *takes* the job and goes home with the paycheck. Be humble if you are called back, and resell the employer on your abilities to do his job well.

You will not salvage every lost opportunity. But so few candidates ever practice good follow-up techniques that you will be among scant competition if you do. And under the right circumstances *you* will grab the job from the jaws of defeat and get the position you really want.

Within you at this moment
is the power to do things
you never dreamed possible.

You know what you are today
but not what you may be tomorrow.

Always look at things as they can be.

You can do anything you wish to do,

have anything you wish to have,

be anything you wish to be.

When you do all the things
you are capable of
you will literally astound yourself.

Chapter 13

60 Seconds & You're Hired!

Real people use these techniques every day. They report that the 60 Second Sell and the 5 Point Agenda were instrumental in landing the job, and easy to create and use. They refer to them as great hiring shortcuts. Seminar participants sigh with relief once they learn my strategies to handle tricky, tough questions using effective, concise answers. Clients repeatedly secure more money when they apply my salary negotiation guidelines. Thousands have used these strategies, and they all have had the same conclusion—the strategies really work. That's why I'm convinced they will work for you.

Let me share a few success stories. No, not the easy cases. I selected the hard ones, those with real life challenges that you could also be facing, to prove these techniques *land* jobs. Our real people include:

Tom—a laid-off, highly paid senior executive
Patricia—a financial executive who wanted to
    change fields
Jeff—a new college grad facing a very competitive
    job market
Linda—handling a divorce and a job change

Don—who wanted to change careers at age 41
Mary—an association director who was fired
Victoria—who wanted a promotion

Tom was a talented chief financial officer who had been highly paid before his company sold the broadcasting business whose financial operations he oversaw. Headhunters had told Tom he was overpaid and needed to expect a $20,000 salary cut. Tom's resumé and targeted cover letter got him an interview with one of the country's top communication companies. This employer conducted nine hours of interviews with Tom over several meetings. Tom felt that the 5 Point Agenda helped him to demonstrate his abilities beyond his financial skills to include his team development, strategic planning, and presentation abilities. The short 60 second answers really got the conversation going. He landed the job, and got a better salary package than he had before by using our negotiations guidelines. Within one year Tom was promoted to director of finance.

Patricia wanted to change fields. She was fascinated with software development, but all her experience had been in retail apparel. She spent hours researching this new field. She wrote to say it was her 60 Second Sell and my advice on answering tough questions that helped her to land her dream job. She's now happily the controller for a growing software company.

Jeff found that a business degree from a good four-year college was not as marketable as he thought it would be. On graduation day no one was standing in line to hire him. He was discouraged by how difficult the job hunt was and how long it was taking him. He had worked construction jobs to help pay for his college education and thus had no applicable experience to land his goal—a position in store management. Jeff and I worked on creating a 5 Point Agenda and a 60 Second Sell that demonstrated his strong work ethic and his ability to work well with all kinds of people. He was amazed that he indeed had important skills to sell an employer. He worked hard developing great answers to the potential questions. Jeff was hired as an assistant store manager for a national paint store. His years in construction helped him to excel in his new career—selling house paint.

Linda was going through a difficult divorce when she got a notice that her employer was closing the branch office where she worked. Her situation was desperate—as the sole supporter of her children, she needed a job. Linda had had 10 interviews and had failed miserably at each.

Linda and I evaluated her strengths. We created her 5 Point Agenda and 60 Second Sell and also worked on answers to difficult questions. After two more interviews, Linda was hired as a loan officer at one of America's top banks.

Don was 41 and hated the high-pressured finance world. He had lost two jobs during corporate restructurings and he had spent 10 months looking for a finance job he didn't want after his last layoff.

Our sessions focused on changing his belief that at 41 he could not enter the retail merchandising world. He was willing to take a salary cut and tried a part-time retail job before officially launching a full-scale job hunt. Together we worked hard to create a 5 Point Agenda and an influential 60 Second Sell. Our sessions role-playing answers to questions using the 60-second approach increased his confidence. Don's new job is in New York City as part of Macy's buying team, and he's had several promotions, with his eye on becoming a store manager; he is quite happy he made the change.

Mary underestimated how difficult her job search would be when she was fired. She bombed during her first interview, easily tripping over the "Why were you let go" questions. Mary secretly worried about whether she was as good as she thought. She feared landing a new position with the type of difficult politics that had been her downfall in her last job. We analyzed Mary's strengths as an association executive director—media, PR, events, conferences, interpersonal abilities, organization, and planning. Her weaknesses were budgets, finance, and trying to please everyone, especially board members with opposing agendas. Our interview sessions restored her self-confidence—I knew she would work again and often told her so. We created a 5 Point Agenda and 60 Second Sell that emphasized her strengths. She investigated the associations to learn which environments offered opportunities to use her strengths, while not relying on her to provide the financial direction she was not skilled at. Lastly, she sought an organization with only one boss where she could achieve the goals that one person set out. She feels that using these techniques allowed her to be selected for an executive director position from among 155 candidates. She's been very successful and happy in her new position.

Victoria spent several years at a large, prominent company. She continued to take on new human resource duties as her job kept expanding. She excelled, but her requests to upgrade her salary seemed to get lost behind other items her boss found more important. Although she performed a management job, her salary remained stuck at $27,000. After six months of promised raises and title changes, her promotion was still not official. So she began to job-hunt. In an early interview she told the hiring manager her true salary. The HR recruiter later told her that once the hiring manager heard the low figure her current employer paid her, the employer changed his opinion of her and her achievements and abilities. (His job paid twice her salary.) During a coaching session, Victoria learned the correct salary negotiation techniques. She applied them when an impressive high-tech company needed a new human resource generalist. Coupled with good answers and solid work examples, she landed the job at $68,000—a 151% pay raise over the job she left.

I've shared my shortcuts and hiring strategies to aid you in communicating to the employer how you can meet his or her needs. That is the key to open your door of opportunity. Just as Victoria, Jeff, and countless others have found good positions, so will you. The 5 Point Agenda is an easy tool to create. It provides you with a clear direction to stress your five major strengths, demonstrating how well you can do the employer's job. The 60 Second Sell is a clever strategy that effectively markets your most important abilities in a short, concise way. You can now write out your answers that, once spoken, will convince the employer to hire you. You know exactly how to negotiate for more salary and benefits in a way that produces results. All you need to do now is put these techniques into action. You too can and will succeed. I know it's just 60 seconds and *you're* hired.